365
VEGETARIAN
STUDENT
COOKBOOK

hamlyn

365
VEGETARIAN
STUDENT
COOKBOOK

Healthy, super-quick dishes for every day of the year

An Hachette UK Company
www.hachette.co.uk

First published in Great Britain in 2020 by Hamlyn,
an imprint of Octopus Publishing Group Ltd
Carmelite House, 50 Victoria Embankment
London EC4Y 0DZ
www.octopusbooks.co.uk

This material was previously published in *Hamlyn All Colour: 200 Really Easy Recipes*
and *Hamlyn QuickCook Vegetarian*.

ISBN 978-0-60063-651-9

A CIP catalogue record for this book is available from the British Library

Printed and bound in China

10 9 8 7 6 5 4 3 2 1

Both metric and imperial measurements are given for the recipes. Use one set of
measures only, not a mixture of both.

Standard level spoon measurements are used in all recipes
1 tablespoon = 15 ml
1 teaspoon = 5 ml

Ovens should be preheated to the specified temperature. If using a fan-assisted
oven, follow the manufacturer's instructions for adjusting the time and temperature.
Grills should also be preheated.

This book includes dishes made with nuts and nut derivatives. It is advisable for those
with known allergic reactions to nuts and nut derivatives and those who may be
potentially vulnerable to these allergies, such as pregnant and nursing mothers,
invalids, the elderly, babies and children, to avoid dishes made with nuts and nut oils.

It is also prudent to check the labels of prepared ingredients for the possible inclusion
of nut derivatives.

Contents

Introduction

30 20 10 – quick, quicker, quickest

This book offers a new and flexible approach to
meal-planning for busy cooks and lets you choose the
recipe option that best fits the time you have available.
Inside you will find 365 dishes that will inspire you and
motivate you to get cooking every day of the year. All
the recipes take a maximum of 30 minutes to cook.
Some take as little as 20 minutes and, amazingly, many
take only 10 minutes. With a bit of preparation, you can
easily try out one new recipe from this book each night
and slowly you will build a wide and exciting portfolio
of recipes to suit your needs.

How does it work?

Every recipe can be cooked one of three ways – a
30-minute version, a 20-minute version or a super-
quick and easy 10-minute version. At the beginning
of each chapter you'll find recipes listed by time. Choose
a dish based on how much time you have and turn to
that page.

You'll find the main recipe in the middle of the page with
a beautiful photograph and two time-variations below.

If you enjoy the dish, you can go back and cook the other time options. If you liked the 20-minute Ravioli with Sweet Potato, Tomatoes and Rocket (see pages 190–191), but only have 10 minutes to spare, then you'll find a way to cook it using cheat ingredients or clever shortcuts.

If you love the ingredients and flavours of the 10-minute Asparagus and Udon Noodle Stir-Fry (see pages 218–219), why not try something more substantial such as the 20-minute Asparagus, Beans and Udon Noodle Bowl, or be inspired to cook a more elaborate meal using similar ingredients, such as Udon Noodle Pancakes with Griddled Asparagus.

Alternatively, browse through all of the 365 delicious recipes, find something that takes your eye, then cook the version that fits your time frame.

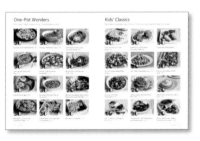

Or, for easy inspiration, turn to the gallery on pages 12–19 to get an instant overview by themes, such as One-Pot Wonders or Kids' Classics.

365 Student Vegetarian

The key to a well-balanced vegetarian diet is simple: eat plenty of wholegrains (such as brown rice, barley, corn, oats, millet and buckwheat), foods which are made from wholegrains (such as wholemeal breads, pastas and cereals), protein-rich pulses, lentils, nuts and eggs, and fresh fruit and vegetables. Dairy products (such as butter, cheese, milk and yogurt) or non-dairy alternatives should form a smaller part of the diet.

Complex carbohydrates are essential for a good diet and vital for energy (such as wholemeal bread, wholewheat pasta, brown rice, barley, corn, dried beans and bananas). Dietary fibre allows the energy from the natural sugars they contain to be released slowly, as opposed to refined sugars, which are released quickly and can leave energy levels depleted.

A healthy vegetarian diet will be high in fibre which is vital for moving the food in the bowel, helping to prevent intestinal problems and reducing the risk of bowel cancer. Foods rich in fibre can help to lower blood cholesterol, therefore it is advisable to include in most meals (such as beans and peas, cabbage, broccoli, Brussels sprouts, oats and wholegrain wheat).

Protein is essential for tissue repair and cell growth and reproduction, especially for growing children and pregnant women. However, we do not need large amounts of protein in our diet and it is perfectly possible to consume the recommended amounts of protein from non-animal foods. Good sources of vegetarian protein include nuts and seeds, pulses, soya products, peas, beans, chickpeas and lentils.

365 Ingredients

The secret to being able to cook speedy meals lies in your store cupboard being well stocked with ingredients that you can use on a day-to-day basis. Remember to check on your stocks regularly and to keep topping them up.

Store Cupboard Staples

Dried pasta (linguini, spaghetti, fusilli, penne and orzo).

Rice (basmati, brown, jasmine, risotto and paella), bulgar wheat, couscous, polenta and quinoa.

Quick-cooking pulses such as Puy lentils, split red lentils and yellow split peas, and canned pulses and beans (including kidney beans, chickpeas, black-eyed beans, cannellini beans).

Nuts and seeds (sunflower seeds, sesame seeds, cashew nuts, almonds, pistachios and walnuts).

Canned tomatoes and passata.

Good-quality olive oil, sunflower and vegetable oils and red wine, white wine, balsamic, cider and rice wine vinegars.

Flavourings

Have a variety of dried herbs and spices in your store cupboard. Buy them in small quantities and use within three months. A good stock of dried herbs (basil, thyme, oregano, tarragon, rosemary and parsley are a good starting point), whole spices (cumin seeds, coriander seeds, black mustard seeds, cloves, cardamom pods and cinnamon sticks) and ground spices (cumin, cinnamon, coriander, chilli powder, paprika and turmeric) will really add depth to your dishes. Sea salt and fresh black peppercorns are also a must.

Soy sauce, sweet chilli sauce, Worcestershire sauce and Tabasco sauce, honey and maple syrup are also useful.

Fresh Food

Keeping your fridge well stocked will enable you to put together healthy and tasty vegetarian meals in minutes. The key is to buy fresh regularly, and to only buy what you know you will use. Fresh pasta, tofu, cheese, butter, milk, cream, eggs, lemons, limes, red chillies, fresh ginger, spring onions and fresh herbs are great to have.

Buy fruit and vegetables that are in season and, if possible, locally grown. Garlic, onions, potatoes, shallots, carrots and other root vegetables and fruit will keep well for a few days.

Crowd pleasers

Need to save some money but fancy a treat? Here are some easy meals and snacks that can be made quickly and cheaply. They are all easy to scale up and can be enjoyed with friends.

1. Garlic bread

Heat a ridged griddle pan until hot, add thick slices of sourdough bread and cook for 2 minutes on each side until lightly charred. Rub each bread slice with a peeled garlic clove and drizzle with extra virgin olive oil.

2. Guacamole

Place a peeled, pitted and diced avocado in a food processor or blender with a crushed garlic clove, seeded and chopped red chilli, juice of a lime, some chopped fresh coriander, and salt and pepper to taste. Process until fairly smooth and transfer to a bowl. Stir in a seeded and finely chopped tomato and serve.

3. Tortilla wedges

Cut large flour tortillas into 12 wedges. Spray with olive oil spray and season one side with salt, pepper and a little cayenne pepper. Lay on a grill rack, spice-side up, and toast under a preheated medium grill for 1–2 minutes until crisp.

4. Avocado, blue cheese & spinach melt

Split a flat roll in half and spread the base with a little butter. Mash together a peeled, pitted, and sliced avocado, some crumbled blue cheese and a little double cream. Spread onto the base of the roll and add a few baby spinach leaves. Top and cook in a dry, hot skillet for 4 minutes on each side or until golden and the cheese has melted.

5. Hummus

Place a tin of chickpeas, drained, a crushed garlic clove, a glug of extra-virgin olive oil, some lemon juice, and salt and pepper to taste in a food processor or blender and process until smooth. Serve with some sticks of carrot and cucumber.

Cheesy Treats

The ultimate comfort food, these cheese-based dishes will satisfy and delight.

Baked Goats' Cheese with Honey and Pistachio 24

Camembert 'Fondue' with Honey and Walnuts 36

Hot-Crumbed Bocconcini with Fresh Pesto and Aïoli 52

Spiced Paneer Bruschettas 56

Watermelon, Olive, Green Bean and Feta Salad 100

Grilled Haloumi, Mixed Peppers and Rocket Salad 116

Romanesco Cauliflower Cheese 156

Smoked Cheese, Pepper and Spinach Quesadillas 164

Asparagus and Fontina Cheese Crespelles 180

Tarragon and Cheddar Cheese Soufflé Omelette 188

Deep-Fried Haloumi Beer-Battered Fritters 192

Broccoli and Blue Cheese Soufflés 210

Pasta and Noodles

Hearty and healthy, pasta and noodles are the ultimate fast food.

Warm Pasta Salad with
Lemon and Broccoli 94

Delicatessen Pasta Salad 102

Creamy Courgette
Orzo Pasta 128

Spinach, Cherry Tomato and
Blue Cheese Pasta Salad 140

Kale and Pecorino Pesto
Linguini 144

Pasta with Asparagus, Beans
and Pesto 148

Rigatoni with Fresh Tomato,
Chilli, Garlic and Basil 152

Tomato and Aubergine
Pappardelle 160

Cold Asian Summer
Soba Noodle Salad 168

Tortellini, Roasted Pepper
and Rocket Salad 170

Tagliatelle with Pumpkin
and Sage 184

Ravioli with Sweet Potato,
Tomatoes and Rocket 190

One-Pot Wonders

When time is short, these one-pot meals will save the day.

Spinach and Potato Tortilla 50

Chunky Mushroom Soup 74

Oriental Rice Soup with
Egg and Greens 84

Spinach and Red Lentil
Soup 86

Greek-Style Summer
Omelette 130

Mixed Bean and Tomato
Chilli 146

Ranch-Style Eggs 150

Spinach Dhal with Cherry
Tomatoes 154

Broccoli and Mushrooms in Black
Bean Sauce with Noodles 182

Malaysian Coconut and
Vegetable Stew 194

Butter Bean and Vegetable
Nut Crumble 222

Blackberry Crumble 236

Kids' Classics

Please the little people in your life with these fruit- and vegetable-filled favourites.

Corn and Bean Tortilla Stack 40

Sweetcorn Cakes with Avocado Salsa 46

Vegetable Spring Rolls 62

Quick Roasted Vegetable Pizzas 124

Stir-Fried Vegetable Rice 158

Pesto and Antipasti Puff Tart 198

Flash-In-The-Pan Ratatouille 200

Spring Onion, Dill and Chive Pancakes 212

Quick Mini Lemon Meringue Pies 230

Berry, Honey and Yogurt Pots 234

French Toast with Blueberries and Redcurrants 246

Chocolate Fondue with a Selection of Dippers 258

Spicy Specials

These tasty dishes will really pack a punch at mealtimes.

Grilled Sweetcorn Cobettes with Herb and Chilli Butter 26

Bulgar Salad with Roasted Peppers on Little Gem 30

Spiced Onion Fritters with Mint and Coriander Relish 38

Chilli, Tomato and Rosemary Beans on Bruschetta 42

Spiced Potato, Coriander and Celeriac Soup 70

Jamaican Spiced Corn Chowder 82

Tex-Mex Sweetcorn Salad 162

Vegetable Pad Thai 186

Nasi Goreng 196

Spicy Szechuan Tofu and Vegetable Stir-Fry 204

Quick Curried Egg Salad 224

Spiced Caramelized Pineapple with Rum 260

Fruity Favourites

Packed with nutritious fruit, here are some delicious ways to your five a day.

Chicory Boats with Gorgonzola, Pear and Walnuts 28

Beetroot and Apple Soup 72

Fruity Potato Salad 106

Couscous Salad with Peppers and Preserved Lemon 110

Quinoa, Courgette and Pomegranate Salad 118

Jewelled Fruity Spicy Pilaf 178

Lemon and Herb Risotto 216

Baked Amaretto Figs 232

Instant Summer Berry Sorbet 248

Peach and Raspberry Cheesecake Pots 254

Watermelon, Lime and Grenadine Squares 268

Lime, Banana and Coconut Fritters 274

Spring Selection

Make the most of everything the season has to offer with these fabulous recipes.

Deluxe Eggs Florentine 32

Lettuce, Pea and Tarragon Soup 76

Iced Green Gazpacho 80

Veggie Caesar-Style Salad with Garlic and Herb Croutons 92

Kachumber and Basmati Rice Salad 108

Green Vegetable Curry 134

Rustic Italian-Style Mushrooms with Soft Polenta 136

Creamy Mushroom and Herb Pancakes 172

Roasted Vegetable Couscous Salad 202

Mixed Berry Eton Mess 252

Rhubarb, Orange and Stem Ginger Pots 256

Luscious Victoria and Strawberry Sponge 264

Autumn Delights

The perfect dishes to brighten up cool autumn days.

Stuffed Aubergine and Yogurt Rolls 34

Creamy Tarragon Mushrooms on Brioche Toast 44

Hearty Minestrone 78

Warm Moroccan Bulgar and Roasted Vegetable Salad 96

Black-Eyed Bean and Red Pepper 'Stew' 126

Beetroot Pasta with Herbs 132

Herby Bulgar and Chickpea Salad 166

Autumnal Moroccan Vegetable Tagine 206

Aubergine and Harissa Sauté 208

Cherry and Vanilla Brûlée 238

Chocolate Fondant Puddings 240

Spiced Drop Scones with Ice Cream and Chocolate Sauce 242

Snacks and Light Bites

Recipes listed by cooking time

10

30 Baked Goats' Cheese with Honey and Pistachio

Serves 4

8 vine leaves, rinsed well in
  cold water
melted butter, for brushing
65 g (2½ oz) pistachio nuts
4 small Crottin de Chèvre
4 teaspoons white wine

For the salad

1 garlic clove, crushed
2 tablespoons cider vinegar
1 tablespoon runny honey
6 tablespoons extra virgin
  olive oil
2 pears, cored and thinly sliced
2 small radicchio, leaves separated
salt and pepper

- Gently dry the vine leaves, then on a clean work surface lay one flat and partly overlap another leaf side by side (by about one-third). Repeat with the other 6 vine leaves; you should end up with 4 pairs. Brush the leaves with a little melted butter and set aside. Whizz the pistachio nuts in a small food processor until coarsely ground.

- Brush the cheeses with the remaining melted butter and then roll them in the chopped pistachios to coat. Place a cheese portion in the centre of each pair of leaves and sprinkle with the wine. Form a parcel by bringing the vine leaves up around each cheese and secure with string or cocktail sticks. Place the cheese parcels on a baking sheet and bake in a preheated oven, 160°C (325°F), Gas Mark 3, for 12–15 minutes.

- Meanwhile, make the salad. Whisk the garlic, vinegar, honey and seasoning together, then gradually whisk in the oil. Toss with the pear and radicchio leaves and set aside.

- Serve the crottins, still in their vine leaf wrappings to be unwrapped at the table, accompanied by the salad.

---

10 Goats' Cheese, Pear and Pistachio Melts

Rub 4 large slices sourdough bread with 2 halved garlic cloves and drizzle each with 1 tablespoon olive oil. Thinly slice 1 pear and arrange over the bread. Sprinkle over 100 g (3½ oz) chopped pistachio nuts and cover with thin slices from 2 small Crottin de Chèvre. Cook under a preheated hot grill for 2–3 minutes or until the cheese is just melting and serve with a radicchio salad.

20 Grilled Goats' Cheese, Pear, Radicchio and Pistachio Salad

Thickly slice a 300 g (10 oz) log goats' cheese, such as Kidderton Ash. Toss 1 head radicchio leaves in 1 tablespoon olive oil and season. Slice 2 pears and arrange with the radicchio on 4 serving plates. Transfer the goats' cheese slices to a sheet of foil and cook under a preheated medium grill for 2 minutes, or until just melted. Divide between the 4 plates, drizzle with 4 tablespoons olive oil and 2 tablespoons cider vinegar. To finish, scatter over 100 g (3½ oz) chopped pistachio nuts and drizzle over 1 tablespoon runny honey. Serve immediately.

Grilled Sweetcorn Cobettes with Herb and Chilli Butter

Serves 4

4 sweetcorn cobs

For the herb and chilli butter

200 g (7 oz) butter, softened
6 tablespoons finely chopped dill
2 red chillies, deseeded and
finely chopped

- Mix together all the ingredients for the herb and chilli butter and set aside.

- Cut each corn cob into 3 equal-sized pieces or cobettes. Insert a wooden or metal skewer into the side of each cobette and place on a barbecue or on a hot griddle pan and cook, turning frequently, for 4–5 minutes or until lightly charred and blistered in places.

- Remove the cobettes from the heat, brush with the butter and serve immediately.

 Speedy Spicy Sweetcorn Chowder Add 400 g (13 oz) fresh sweetcorn kernels to a saucepan with 4 sliced spring onions, 1 deseeded and finely chopped red chilli, 100 ml (3½ fl oz) double cream and 500 ml (17 fl oz) vegetable stock. Bring to the boil, stir in 2 tablespoons chopped coriander and serve immediately.

 Sweetcorn and Herb Frittata Lightly beat 6 eggs in a bowl, season and add 2 tablespoons each of chopped coriander, dill and mint. Heat 2 tablespoons olive oil in a medium, nonstick frying pan and add ½ small chopped onion, 1 deseeded and finely chopped red chilli and 2 crushed garlic cloves. Stir-fry for 3–4 minutes and then toss in 400 g (13 oz) fresh sweetcorn kernels and stir-fry for a further 2–3 minutes. Pour over the egg mixture and cook over a medium heat for 10 minutes or until the base is set. Place the frying pan under a preheated medium grill for 4–5 minutes or until the top is set and golden. Remove from the heat, cut into wedges and serve.

Chicory Boats with Gorgonzola, Pear and Walnuts

Serves 4

1 ripe pear, cored and finely chopped

2 tablespoons crème fraîche

65 g (2½ oz) Gorgonzola cheese, crumbled

20 red or green Belgian chicory leaves (or a mixture of both)

25 g (1 oz) walnuts, toasted and roughly chopped

olive oil, to drizzle

- Mix together the pear, crème fraîche and Gorgonzola in a small bowl.

- Arrange the chicory leaves on a serving platter and spoon a little of the pear mixture on to the base of each leaf.

- Sprinkle the chopped nuts over the top of the filling, drizzle with a little olive oil, and serve.

 Braised Chicory and Beans with Gorgonzola Cut 4 heads chicory lengthways into quarters, but do not trim off the base. Melt 100 g (3½ oz) butter in a large frying pan, add the chicory and cook for 4–5 minutes, turning occasionally, until golden. Add 2 thinly sliced leeks, a 400 g (13 oz) can butter beans, drained, 200 ml (7 fl oz) hot vegetable stock, 2 teaspoons sugar, 100 g (3½ oz) crumbled Gorgonzola cheese and 4 tablespoons crème fraîche. Bring to the boil, cover and simmer for 6–8 minutes. Turn the chicory over, increase the heat and cook for a further 1–2 minutes until the leeks are tender and the gravy has thickened. Serve immediately with crusty bread.

 Baked Chicory and Gorgonzola Trim any coarse or bruised outer leaves from 8 large heads red chicory. Place in a baking dish into which they will fit snugly in a single layer. Drizzle over 6 tablespoons olive oil and season to taste. Scatter over 100 g (3½ oz) crumbled Gorgonzola cheese and the juice of 1 lemon. Bake in a preheated oven, 180°C (350°F), Gas Mark 4, for 20 minutes. Serve straight from the baking dish with the juices and scatter over 4 tablespoons chopped toasted walnuts before serving.

30 Bulgar Salad with Roasted Peppers on Little Gem

Serves 4

200 g (7 oz) fine-ground
bulgar wheat
1 tablespoon tomato purée
juice of 1½ lemons
5 tablespoons extra virgin
olive oil
1 red chilli, finely chopped
200 g (7 oz) roasted red peppers
(from a jar), drained and diced
8 spring onions, finely sliced
300 g (10 oz) tomatoes, diced
50 g (2 oz) flat leaf parsley,
roughly chopped
25 g (1 oz) mint leaves,
roughly chopped
4 little gem lettuces,
leaves separated
salt

· Tip the bulgar wheat into a bowl, pour over 125 ml (4 fl oz) boiling water, stir, then cover and leave for 10–15 minutes until the grains are tender.

· Add the tomato purée, lemon juice, olive oil, the red chilli and some salt to the bulgar wheat mixture and mix thoroughly.

· Add the roasted red peppers, spring onions and tomatoes, together with the parsley and mint, and mix well.

· Arrange the lettuce leaves around the edges of a platter with the bulgar salad in the centre. Use the leaves to scoop up the bulgar mixture and eat.

10 **Roasted Red Pepper, Marinated Vegetable and Bulgar Salad**
Prepare the bulgar wheat mixture as above and place in a salad bowl. Drain the oil from 200 g (7 oz) chargrilled aubergines, roasted red peppers and mushrooms (from a jar) and add to the bulgar wheat. Finish off with 1 chopped red chilli and 4 tablespoons chopped flat leaf parsley, toss to mix well and serve.

20 **Layered Roasted Red Pepper, Bulgar and Tomato Pot** Prepare the bulgar wheat mixture as above and tip into a medium-sized shallow ovenproof dish with 200 g (7 oz) diced roasted red pepper (from a jar), drained. Slice 4 plum tomatoes and place over the bulgar wheat to cover. Sprinkle over 1 finely chopped red chilli and drizzle over 4 tablespoons olive oil. Cook under a preheated medium grill for 5 minutes. Crumble 150 g (5 oz) feta cheese on top and scatter over 8 chopped pitted black olives. Return the dish to the grill for 4–5 minutes or until the feta is browned. Serve immediately.

30 Deluxe Eggs Florentine

Serves 4

12 asparagus spears, trimmed
2 tablespoons butter, plus extra
  for buttering
150 g (5 oz) baby spinach
pinch of freshly grated nutmeg
2 English muffins, halved and
  lightly toasted
1 tablespoon vinegar
4 large eggs
8 tablespoons ready-made
  hollandaise sauce, to serve
salt and pepper

- Blanch the asparagus spears in a pan of boiling water for 2–3 minutes, drain and keep warm.

- Meanwhile, melt the butter in a large frying pan, add the spinach and stir-fry for 3 minutes or until just wilted. Season with grated nutmeg, salt and black pepper.

- Split and toast the muffins, and butter them just before serving.

- Poach the eggs by bringing a saucepan of lightly salted water to the boil. Add the vinegar and reduce to a gentle simmer. Swirl the water with a fork and crack 2 of the eggs into the water. Cook for 3–4 minutes, remove carefully with a slotted spoon and repeat with the remaining 2 eggs.

- Meanwhile, heat the hollandaise sauce according to the packet instructions.

- Top the toasted muffins with some spinach and a poached egg and spoon over the hollandaise. Sprinkle with freshly ground black pepper and serve each egg with 3 asparagus spears on the side.

---

10 Warm Asparagus Salad with Sunny Side Eggs Cook 500 g (1 lb) trimmed asparagus in lightly salted boiling water for 4–5 minutes. Drain and place in a wide bowl with 4 tablespoons olive oil, season and toss to mix well. Meanwhile, fry 4 eggs in a large nonstick frying pan for 2–3 minutes. Divide the asparagus between 4 warmed plates, sprinkle 1 tablespoon grated Parmesan over each portion and top with a fried egg. Serve immediately.

20 Spinach, Asparagus and Egg Tortilla Beat 6 eggs together with 12 torn basil leaves and season well. Heat 2 tablespoons olive oil in a large frying pan and add the egg mixture. Roughly chop a large handful of baby spinach leaves, 12 asparagus spears and 1 tomato. Scatter the spinach, asparagus and tomatoes evenly over the egg. Cook the tortilla for about 6–8 minutes without stirring and then place under a preheated medium grill for 3–4 minutes or until golden brown all over. Cut the tortilla into wedges and serve with a green salad.

30 Stuffed Aubergine and Yogurt Rolls

Serves 4

1 garlic clove, crushed

3 tablespoons Greek yogurt

200 g (7 oz) feta cheese, crumbled

6 tablespoons finely chopped oregano leaves

2 aubergines

olive oil, for brushing and drizzling

50 g (2 oz) Sunblush tomatoes

a handful basil leaves

salt and pepper

- In a bowl combine the garlic, yogurt, feta and the oregano. Stir well, season to taste and set aside.

- Meanwhile slice the aubergines into slices 5 mm (¼ in) thick. Put a griddle pan over a high heat, brush the aubergine slices with a little oil and griddle, in batches, until they begin to char and soften.

- Spread each aubergine slice with the yogurt mixture and top with a basil leaf and a Sunblush tomato. Roll the slices up, garnish with basil leaves, drizzle over a little olive oil and serve.

---

10 Stuffed Courgette Rolls

Replace the aubergines with 2 large courgettes and grill as in the recipe above. Replace the oregano with chopped mint leaves and the Sunblush tomatoes with 50 g (2 oz) roasted red pepper (from a jar) sliced into strips, and garnish with mint leaves.

20 Aubergine, Feta and Couscous

Salad Grill the aubergines as in the recipe above. Meanwhile place 150 g (5 oz) couscous in a bowl and just cover with boiling water. Cover and allow to stand for 10 minutes or until the liquid is completely absorbed. Cut the aubergine into bite-sized pieces and place in a salad bowl with the couscous, 50 g (2 oz) Sunblush tomatoes, a small handful of basil leaves and 200 g (7 oz) cubed feta cheese. Drizzle over 3 tablespoons of olive oil and serve at room temperature.

Camembert 'Fondue' with Honey and Walnuts

Serves 4

1 small Camembert cheese,
  in a lidded box
6 walnut halves, roughly chopped
2 tablespoons thyme leaves, plus
  extra time sprigs, to garnish
2 tablespoons runny honey
crusty bread and vegetable
  crudités, to serve

- Remove the cheese from its box and discard any paper or plastic wrapping. Slice off the top rind and replace the cheese in its box.

- Sprinkle the surface of the cheese with the walnuts and thyme, and drizzle with the honey.

- Replace the lid and place the box in the centre of a preheated oven, 220°C (425°F), Gas Mark 7, for 5–10 minutes. Depending on the ripeness of the cheese, it should be nicely runny inside when cooked.

- Garnish with thyme sprigs and serve warm with crusty bread and vegetable crudités.

 Camembert, Walnut and Grilled Tomato Open Sandwich Lightly toast 4 large slices sourdough bread and spread each with a teaspoon Dijon mustard. Slice 2 plum tomatoes and lay on top of the mustard. Place 2 slices Camembert cheese over each piece of toast and place under a preheated medium grill for 2–3 minutes or until bubbling. Scatter over 2 tablespoons chopped walnuts and serve immediately with a salad.

 Camembert and Walnut Pasta Cook 375 g (12 oz) penne according to the packet instructions. Drain and keep warm. Meanwhile finely slice 2 garlic cloves and 4 spring onions and stir-fry in a tablespoon olive oil in a large frying pan for 1–2 minutes. Add 2 chopped tomatoes and stir-fry for 5–6 minutes over a medium heat. Finely chop 2 tablespoons tarragon and add to the tomato mixture. Tip the drained pasta into the pan with 200 g (7 oz) chopped Camembert cheese and 100 g (3½ oz) chopped toasted walnuts, and stir to mix well. Season and serve ladled into warmed bowls.

30 Spiced Onion Fritters with Mint and Coriander Relish

Serves 4

3–4 onions, sliced
1 teaspoon red chilli powder
1 teaspoon ground turmeric
2 teaspoons cumin seeds
1 tablespoon coriander seeds, crushed
250 g (8 oz) chickpea flour
vegetable oil, for deep-frying
sea salt

For the relish

8 tablespoons finely chopped mint leaves
6 tablespoons finely chopped coriander leaves
250 ml (8 fl oz) natural yogurt, whisked
1 tablespoon lime juice
1 tablespoon mint jelly

- First make the relish by mixing all the ingredients together in a bowl, season well and chill until ready to serve.

- Separate the sliced onions in a large bowl. Add the chilli powder, turmeric, cumin seeds, crushed coriander seeds and season with sea salt. Mix well. Add the chickpea flour a little at a time, stirring again to coat the onions. Now gradually sprinkle some cold water over this mixture, adding just enough water to make quite a sticky batter that coats the onions. Use your fingers to mix thoroughly.

- Fill a deep, wide saucepan one-quarter full with vegetable oil and place over a high heat until it reaches 180°C (350°F) or a cube of bread sizzles and turns golden in 10–15 seconds.

- Drop spoonfuls of the mixture into the oil. Fry in batches over medium–high heat for 1–2 minutes or until golden brown and crisp on the outside. Remove with a slotted spoon and drain on kitchen paper. Serve immediately with the relish.

10 Spiced Fried Okra

Place 65 g (2½ oz) chickpea flour in a bowl. Slice 400 g (13 oz) okra lengthwise into quarters and toss in the flour. Pour vegetable oil into a large saucepan to a depth of 2.5 cm (1 in) and heat until a breadcrumb sizzles gently when placed in the oil. Fry the okra until crisp and golden brown, stirring occasionally. Remove with a slotted spoon and transfer to a bowl lined with kitchen paper. Sprinkle over 1 teaspoon each of salt, chilli powder and dried mango powder and toss well. Serve hot with naan bread.

20 Spiced Chickpea Flour Pancakes

Tip 150 g (5 oz) chickpea flour into a mixing bowl. Slowly add 250 ml (8 fl oz) water, mixing to a smooth batter. Add ½ teaspoon each of salt, cayenne pepper and cumin seeds, 1 finely chopped red onion, 1 teaspoon grated ginger, 4 finely chopped green chillies, 4 chopped garlic cloves and 2 tablespoons chopped coriander leaves. Smear a large nonstick frying pan with 1 teaspoon vegetable oil using kitchen paper and set over a medium heat. When hot, stir the batter and pour about 50 ml (2 fl oz) into the centre of the pan. Quickly tilt the pan in all directions, spreading the batter to make an 18–19 cm (7–7½ in) diameter pancake. Cover and cook for 3 minutes or until the pancake is reddish-brown at the bottom. Dribble another teaspoon of oil around the edges of the pancake. Turn it over and cook, uncovered, for a further minute or until golden. Remove from the heat and cover with a plate. Repeat with the remaining batter to make 8 pancakes. Serve immediately with yogurt and mango chutney.

30 Corn and Bean Tortilla Stack

Serves 4

2 red peppers, deseeded
   and chopped
2 tablespoons olive oil
1 x 400 g (13 oz) can chopped
   tomatoes
2 x 400 g (13 oz) cans kidney
   beans, drained
2 x 200 g (7 oz) cans sweetcorn,
   drained
½ teaspoon chilli powder
4 large corn tortillas
200g (7 oz) Cheddar cheese,
   grated
1 tablespoon finely chopped
   coriander leaves, to garnish

To serve

soured cream (optional)
1 avocado, peeled, stoned
   and sliced (optional)

- Place the chopped peppers and olive oil in a large pan, cover and cook gently for 5 minutes. Add the tomatoes, beans, sweetcorn and chilli powder. Bring to the boil and simmer, uncovered, for 7–8 minutes until the mixture is quite thick.

- Place 1 tortilla on a baking sheet. Top with one-third of the bean mixture and one-quarter of the cheese. Repeat this twice to make 3 layers and then place the final tortilla on top. Sprinkle with the remaining cheese and bake in a preheated oven, 190°C (375°F), Gas Mark 5, for 15 minutes.

- Garnish with the chopped coriander leaves and serve with avocado and soured cream, if desired.

10 Bean and Corn Wraps

Spread 4 corn tortillas with 2 tablespoons mayonnaise each. Mix together sweetcorn from a 200 g (7 oz) can and 8 tablespoons kidney beans. Divide this mixture over the tortillas and sprinkle each with a tablespoon grated Cheddar cheese. Roll up the tortillas to encase the filling and serve.

20 Spicy Tortilla Crisps with a Creamy Bean Dip

Take 4 corn tortillas and cut each one into 12 wedges. Place on a large baking sheet and drizzle with a little olive oil and sprinkle over 2 teaspoons cumin seeds and 2 teaspoons smoked paprika. Bake in a preheated oven, 180°C (350°F), Gas Mark 4, for 8–10 minutes or until crisp.

Meanwhile make the dip. Drain and rinse the beans from 2 x 400 g (13 oz) cans kidney beans and tip into a food processor along with 2 crushed garlic cloves, 6 tablespoons finely chopped parsley, 200 g (7 oz) soft cheese with garlic and herbs and blend until smooth. Season and serve with the tortilla crisps.

 # Chilli, Tomato and Rosemary Cannellini Beans on Bruschetta

Serves 4

3 tablespoons extra virgin olive
oil, plus extra for drizzling

2 teaspoons chopped
rosemary leaves

1 red chilli, chopped

2 x 400 g (13 oz) cans cannellini
beans, drained

2 tablespoons chopped Sunblush
tomatoes

8 slices day-old bread from
a sourdough loaf

2 garlic cloves, halved

sea salt and pepper

To garnish

basil leaves

lemon wedges

- Heat the oil in a frying pan over a low heat. Add the rosemary leaves and chilli and cook for a few seconds, until the mixture starts to sizzle. Add the beans and stir-fry for 2–3 minutes.

- Transfer to a food processor and whizz until roughly combined. Season to taste with sea salt and pepper and fold in the chopped tomatoes.

- Heat a griddle pan and warm the bread slices over a medium–high heat until lightly charred, or toast in a toaster. Rub the warm bread with the garlic halves and drizzle generously with olive oil. Sprinkle lightly with sea salt and top with the bean mixture.

- Sprinkle with freshly ground black pepper and lightly drizzle again with oil. Garnish with basil leaves and lemon wedges.

 ### Tomato and Chilli Bean Soup

Heat 2 x 400 g (13 oz) cans of cream of tomato soup and stir in 1 finely chopped red chilli and a 400 g (13 oz) can cannellini beans, drained and rinsed. Bring to the boil and serve piping hot with toasted sourdough bread.

 ### Vegetable and Cannellini Bean

Gratin Cook 2 x 250 g (8 oz) packs prepared vegetables (cauliflower, carrots and broccoli, for instance) in a large saucepan of boiling water for 3–4 minutes. Drain and transfer to a shallow ovenproof dish and mix with 400 g (13 oz) tub ready-made tomato pasta sauce and 400 g (13 oz) can cannellini beans, drained and rinsed.

Mix together 200 g (7 oz) fresh breadcrumbs with 100 g (3½oz) grated Parmesan cheese and sprinkle over the vegetable mixture. Bake in a preheated oven, 200°C (400°F), Gas Mark 6, for 15–20 minutes until bubbling and golden. Serve immediately.

Creamy Tarragon Mushrooms on Brioche Toasts

Serves 4

8 slices brioche
150 g (5 oz) butter
2 banana shallots, finely chopped
3 garlic cloves, finely chopped
1 red chilli, deseeded and finely chopped (optional)
300 g (10 oz) mixed wild mushrooms (such as chanterelle, cep, girolle and oyster), trimmed and sliced
4 tablespoons crème fraîche, plus extra to garnish (optional)
2 tablespoons finely chopped tarragon
1 tablespoon finely chopped flat leaf parsley
salt and pepper

- Lightly toast the brioche slices and keep warm.

- Heat the butter in a frying pan and sauté the shallots, garlic and chilli, if using, for 1–2 minutes. Now add the mushrooms and stir-fry over a moderate heat for 6–8 minutes. Season well, remove from the heat and stir in the crème fraîche and chopped herbs.

- Spoon the mushrooms on to the sliced brioche and serve immediately, with an extra dollop of crème fraîche if desired.

10 Chunky Mushroom and Tarragon Soup

Heat 2 x 400 g (13 oz) cans of cream of mushroom soup in a saucepan along with 2 x 300 g (10 oz) cans whole button mushrooms. Bring to the boil and simmer for 2–3 minutes until piping hot. Stir in 25 g (1 oz) chopped tarragon and serve immediately, garnished with a little chopped flat leaf parsley.

30 Mushroom and Tarragon Risotto

Bring 1.2 litres (2 pints) vegetable stock to the boil and keep hot. Meanwhile, heat 2 tablespoons olive oil in a large, heavy-based saucepan and add 1 chopped onion and 2 chopped garlic cloves. Fry over a gentle heat for 2–3 minutes, until softened. Add 250 g (8 oz) mixed wild mushrooms (as above) and fry for a further 2–3 minutes, until browned. Stir in 375 g (12 oz) arborio rice and stir to coat with the oil. Pour over 150 ml (¼ pint) dry white wine and simmer, stirring, until the liquid has been absorbed. Add a ladleful of the hot stock and simmer, stirring again, until the liquid has been absorbed. Continue adding the stock in this way, until all the liquid has been absorbed and the rice is plump and tender. Finish by stirring in 2 tablespoons each of chopped tarragon and parsley, and 40 g (1½ oz) butter. Season well and serve with freshly grated Parmesan.

30 Sweetcorn Cakes with Avocado Salsa

Serves 4

500 g (1 lb) fresh sweetcorn
kernels
4 spring onions, finely sliced
2 eggs
5 tablespoons finely chopped
coriander leaves, plus extra
to garnish
125 g (4 oz) plain flour
1 teaspoon baking powder
salt and pepper
vegetable oil, for frying

For the avocado salsa

2 ripe avocados, peeled,
stoned and finely diced
4 tablespoons each of chopped
mint and coriander leaves
2 tablespoons lime juice
2 tablespoons finely chopped
red onion
½ teaspoon Tabasco sauce

- Place three-quarters of the sweetcorn kernels along with the spring onions, eggs, coriander, flour and baking powder in a food processor and whizz until combined. Season well and transfer to a large bowl. Add the remaining sweetcorn kernels and mix well.

- Heat 1 tablespoon of vegetable oil in a large nonstick frying pan over a medium–high heat. When the oil is hot, drop heaped tablespoons of the mixture into the pan and cook in batches for 1 minute on each side.

- Drain the sweetcorn cakes on kitchen paper and keep warm in a preheated oven, 120°C (250°F), Gas Mark ½, while making the rest of the cakes.

- To make the avocado salsa, place all the ingredients in a bowl and stir very gently to combine.

- Serve the warm sweetcorn cakes accompanied by the tangy avocado salsa and garnished with coriander leaves.

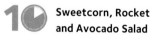 **Sweetcorn, Rocket and Avocado Salad**

Cut each sweetcorn cake into quarters and place in a salad bowl with the avocado salsa. Stir in 75 g (3 oz) rocket leaves and drizzle over 4 tablespoons olive oil. Toss gently to mix well and serve.

 Pea and Mint Fritters

Replace the sweetcorn in the recipe above with thawed frozen peas and the coriander with chopped mint leaves and proceed as above. Stir 6 tablespoons natural yogurt into the salsa and serve with the pea and mint fritters.

1 ⏱ Greek Salad with Toasted Pitta

Serves 4

100 g (3½ oz) feta cheese,
  crumbled into smallish chunks
8–10 fresh mint leaves, shredded
100 g (3½ oz) kalamata olives,
  pitted
2 tomatoes, chopped
juice of a large lemon
1 small red onion, thinly sliced
1 teaspoon dried oregano
4 pitta breads
lemon wedges, to serve

- In a bowl, toss together the feta, mint, olives, tomatoes, lemon juice, onion and oregano.

- Toast the pittas under a preheated hot grill until lightly golden, then split open and toast the open sides.

- Tear the hot pittas into bite-sized pieces, then toss with the other ingredients in the bowl. Serve with lemon wedges.

2 ⏱ Grilled Feta, Spinach and Pine Nut Salad

Place 200 g (7 oz) block feta cheese on a baking sheet and sprinkle over 1 teaspoon dried oregano. Place under a preheated hot grill for 5–6 minutes or until lightly browned. Meanwhile put 300 g (10 oz) of baby spinach in a wide bowl with 1 sliced red onion, 2 chopped tomatoes and 4 tablespoons toasted pine nuts. Sprinkle over 2 tablespoons sherry vinegar then drizzle with 6 tablespoons olive oil. Season well and toss. Cut the grilled feta into small cubes, scatter over the salad and serve.

3 ⏱ Pasta with Mint, Olive and Feta Pesto and Roasted Vegetables

Place 1 red and 1 yellow pepper, deseeded and cut into 2.5 cm (1 in) pieces, 1 medium aubergine, cut into 2.5 cm (1 in) pieces, 1 courgette, cut into 2.5 cm (1 in) cubes and 2 small red onions, peeled and cut into wedges, on a large nonstick baking tray. Drizzle with a little olive oil and season well. Roast in a preheated oven, 200°C (400°F), Gas Mark 6, for 15–20 minutes, or until the edges of the vegetables are just starting to char. Meanwhile, bring a large pan of salted water to the boil. Cook 375 g (12 oz) of rigatoni in the water, according to the packet instructions. Toast 100 g (3½ oz) pine nuts for 4–5 minutes in a dry frying pan until golden brown, stirring often to prevent them from burning. Transfer to a food processor with 200 ml (7 fl oz) olive oil, 4 chopped garlic cloves, 25 g (1 oz) each of chopped mint and basil leaves and 150 g (5 oz) chopped feta to make a coarse pesto. Check the seasoning. Drain the cooked pasta, return to the pan with the roasted vegetables and 100 g (3½ oz) pitted kalamata olives and stir in the pesto. Serve immediately.

3○ Spinach and Potato Tortilla

Serves 4

3 tablespoons olive oil
2 onions, finely chopped
250 g (8 oz) cooked potatoes,
  peeled and cut into 1 cm
  (½ in) cubes
2 garlic cloves, finely chopped
200 g (7 oz) cooked spinach,
  drained thoroughly and
  roughly chopped
4 tablespoons finely chopped
  roasted red pepper
5 eggs, lightly beaten
3–4 tablespoons grated
  Manchego cheese
salt and pepper

- Heat the oil in a nonstick frying pan and add the onions and potatoes. Cook gently over a medium heat for 3–4 minutes or until the vegetables have softened but not coloured, turning and stirring often.

- Add the garlic, spinach and peppers and stir to mix well.

- Beat the eggs lightly and season well. Pour into the frying pan, shaking the pan so that the egg is evenly spread. Cook gently for 8–10 minutes or until the tortilla is set at the bottom.

- Sprinkle over the grated Manchego. Place the frying pan under a preheated medium-hot grill and cook for 3–4 minutes or until the top is set and golden.

- Remove from the heat, cut into bite-sized squares or triangles and serve warm or at room temperature.

1○ Spinach and Potato Sauté

Heat 1 tablespoon vegetable oil in a large frying pan. Add 2 chopped garlic cloves, 1 finely chopped onion and 1 tablespoon curry powder. Stir in 100 ml (3½ fl oz) passata, 300 g (10 oz) baby leaf spinach and 200 g (7 oz) cooked, cubed potatoes. Sauté over a high heat for 2–3 minutes or until piping hot. Season and serve with crusty bread or rice.

2○ Spanish and Potato Stew

Heat 2 tablespoons olive oil in a saucepan and add 4 crushed garlic cloves, 1 chopped onion, 1 finely chopped red pepper, 500 g (1 lb) chopped fresh spinach leaves and 2 medium potatoes that have been cut into 1 cm (½ in) cubes. Add 1 litre (1¾ pints) hot vegetable stock and a pinch of saffron threads. Bring to the boil and cook for 12–15 minutes or until the potatoes are tender. Season and serve with crusty bread or rice.

 # Hot-Crumbed Bocconcini with Fresh Pesto Aïoli

Serves 4

100 g (3½ oz) fresh white breadcrumbs

zest of 1 lemon, finely grated

generous pinch of chilli flakes

2 tablespoons fresh thyme leaves

50 g (2 oz) plain flour

2 large eggs, beaten

300 g (10 oz) bocconcini (baby mozzarella balls), drained

vegetable oil, for deep-frying

salt and pepper

For the fresh pesto aïoli

6 tablespoons fresh ready-made green pesto

200 g (7 oz) fresh mayonnaise

2 garlic cloves, crushed

- Make the pesto aïoli by mixing together all the ingredients. Set aside.

- In a medium bowl, mix together the breadcrumbs, lemon zest, a few chilli flakes, a sprinkling of the thyme and some seasoning. Place the flour in a second bowl and the eggs in a third.

- Pat the mozzarella balls dry with kitchen paper. Roll the balls first in flour, then dip in the egg, then roll in the breadcrumb mixture. Repeat in the egg and breadcrumbs to create a double layer.

- Half fill a saucepan or deep-fat fryer with vegetable oil. Just before serving, heat over a high heat until it reaches 180°C (350°F) or a cube of bread sizzles and turns golden in 10–15 seconds. Using a spider strainer or slotted spoon, lower the crumbed mozzarella into the hot oil and fry for 3–4 minutes until golden brown. Remove and drain on kitchen paper.

- Serve immediately with the fresh pesto aïoli.

 Tomato, Bocconcini and Basil Tricolore Salad Slice 4 tomatoes and place in a wide salad bowl with a small handful basil leaves and 300 g (10 oz) bocconcini. Drizzle over 4 tablespoons extra virgin olive oil and squeeze over the juice of 1 lemon. Season well and serve with ciabatta bread.

Pasta, Boccacino and Pesto Gratin Cook 375 g (12 oz) penne pasta according to the packet instructions. Meanwhile heat 500 ml (17 fl oz) milk until bubbling. Place 3 tablespoons cornflour in a small dish and pour over 6 tablespoons of the hot milk. Mix together to form a paste and return to the milk pan. Stir the milk over a low heat until it starts to thicken. Add 150 g (5 oz) chopped bocconcini and season well with salt, black pepper and grated nutmeg. Stir in 4 tablespoons fresh green pesto. In a separate pan, wilt 75 g (3 oz) spinach and strain out all the liquid. Drain the pasta and add to the cheese sauce. Mix in the spinach and a pinch of dried chilli flakes and transfer to an ovenproof gratin dish. Sprinkle over 50 g (2 oz) grated mozzarella and place under a hot grill for 5 minutes or until golden and bubbling. Serve immediately.

30 Potato Blinis with Beetroot and Chives

Serves 4

200 g (7 oz) ready-made
mashed potato
50 g (2 oz) self-raising flour
3 large eggs, separated
2 tablespoons soured cream
4 tablespoons finely chopped dill
salt and pepper

For the topping

2 cooked beetroot, peeled and
finely diced
6 tablespoons crème fraîche
1 tablespoon creamed horseradish
salt and pepper
chopped chives, to garnish

- Place the mashed potato in a mixing bowl. Beat in the flour, egg yolks, soured cream and dill and season well.

- Whisk the egg whites until stiff. Using a metal spoon, carefully fold the beaten egg whites into the potato mixture.

- Heat a little oil in a large, nonstick frying pan. Add 3–4 separate tablespoons of the potato blini mixture. Fry over medium heat until set, then turn the potato blinis over and fry briefly so that both sides are lightly browned. Remove and keep warm. Repeat the process until all the potato mixture has been used.

- Meanwhile mix together the beetroot, crème fraîche and creamed horseradish and season well.

- To serve, spoon the beetroot mixture over the blinis, garnish with chopped chives and freshly ground black pepper.

10 Beetroot and Chive Colcannon

Blanch 50 g (2 oz) finely shredded curly kale in boiling water for 1 minute. Drain and reserve. Finely chop 50 g (2 oz) chives and coarsely grate 2 cooked beetroots. Place in a food processor with the drained kale and pulse for 10–15 seconds. Meanwhile cook 2 x 400 g (13 oz) packs ready-made mashed potato according to the packet instructions and transfer to a mixing bowl. Add the kale mixture and 1 tablespoon wholegrain mustard. Season and mix well. Serve piping hot with steamed vegetables of your choice.

20 Potato and Chive Soup

Melt 2 tablespoons butter in a saucepan. When it begins to foam, add 1 diced onion and toss in the butter until well coated. Stir in 425 g (14 oz) ready-made mashed potato and 900 ml (1½ pints) hot vegetable stock. Bring to the boil and add the 125 ml (4 fl oz) milk. Purée the soup with a hand-held blender. Season to taste. Stir in 3 tablespoons each very finely chopped dill and chives. Season and serve immediately with crusty bread.

1⃝ Spiced Paneer Bruschettas

Serves 4

200 g (7 oz) fresh paneer
(Indian cheese) or feta cheese,
roughly chopped

3 tablespoons finely chopped
red onion

1 green chilli, deseeded and
finely sliced

large handful fresh coriander,
finely chopped

150 g (5 oz) baby plum tomatoes,
quartered

2 tablespoons extra virgin olive oil,
plus extra for drizzling (optional)

juice and finely grated zest
of 1 lime

12 slices ciabatta bread

salt and pepper

- Place the cheese in a mixing bowl. Add the onions, chilli, coriander, tomatoes, olive oil, lime juice and zest and then season. Stir well and allow to sit while you toast or griddle the ciabatta slices.

- Spoon the cheese mixture over the toasted ciabatta slices and serve immediately, drizzled with extra olive oil if desired.

2⃝ Spiced Paneer Skewers

Cut 500 g (1 lb) paneer into 5 cm (2 in) cubes. Sprinkle with 1 tablespoon each of chilli powder and sea salt. Toss everything together and ensure the paneer is evenly coated. Combine 2 tablespoons chickpea flour with 2 teaspoons cumin seeds and 6 tablespoons double cream. Coat the cubes in the spiced cream and marinate for 10 minutes. Thread on to 4 metal skewers and cook under a preheated hot grill for 1–2 minutes on each side. Serve garnished with chopped coriander leaves and a salad.

3⃝ Palak Paneer (Spinach with Indian Cheese)

Cook 250 g (8 oz) basmati rice according to the packet instructions. Blanch 750 g (1½ lb) baby spinach leaves in boiling water for 1–2 minutes or until wilted. Drain in a colander and run cold water over until cool. Whizz to a smooth paste in a food processor or blender, and set aside. Heat 3 tablespoons vegetable oil in a large nonstick pan. Add 2 teaspoons cumin seeds and fry for about 30 seconds until fragrant, then add 1 chopped onion and fry again over a low heat for about 5–6 minutes, until soft. Add 1 tablespoon each of grated ginger and garlic and 1 chopped green chilli and cook for a further minute. Add 2 teaspoons ground coriander and salt to taste. Cook for a further 30 seconds then add the spinach and 250 g (8 oz) cubed paneer, ½ teaspoon garam masala and 4 tablespoons double cream. Stir and cook for a few minutes longer or until the spinach is nice and creamy. Stir in the juice of 1 lemon to taste. Serve with the cooked rice.

 # Spring Onion Rostis with Avocado, Red Onion and Tomato Salsa

Serves 4

875 g (1¾ lb) boiled potatoes (King Edward or Maris Piper)

6 spring onions, finely chopped

2 garlic cloves, very finely chopped

1 large egg, lightly beaten

4 tablespoons sunflower oil

For the salsa

2 plum tomatoes, deseeded and roughly chopped

1 red chilli, deseeded and finely chopped

1 small red onion, halved and very thinly sliced

4 tablespoons finely chopped fresh coriander

2 avocados, peeled, stoned and roughly diced

juice of 2 limes

1 tablespoon avocado oil

lime wedges, to serve

- First make the salsa by mixing all the ingredients together in a bowl. Season well and set aside until ready to serve.

- Peel and coarsely grate the potatoes. Add the spring onions, garlic and egg and use your fingers to combine evenly.

- Heat a large, nonstick frying pan over a high heat and add half of the oil.

- Working in batches, divide the potato mixture into 8 portions. Spoon 4 of the portions in to the oil and pat down to form rostis about 8–10 cm (3¼–4 in) in diameter. Cook for 3–4 minutes on each side and then carefully transfer to a large nonstick baking sheet. Repeat with the remaining oil and potato mixture to make 8 rostis.

- Serve the rostis accompanied the salsa and the lime wedges.

 ### Spring Onion and Potato Broth

Place 12 sliced spring onions, 400 g (13 oz) cooked, cubed potatoes, 2 crushed garlic cloves, 4 tablespoons chopped coriander leaves, 600 ml (1 pint) hot vegetable stock and 500 ml (17 fl oz) milk in a saucepan. Bring to the boil and cook for 5–6 minutes or until piping hot. Season and serve immediately.

 ### Fresh Salsa and Pasta Salad

Cook 300 g (10 oz) short-shaped pasta according to the packet instructions. Meanwhile finely chop 4 plum tomatoes, 1 red chilli, 1 red onion and 6 tablespoons coriander leaves and place in a wide bowl. Peel, stone and roughly dice 2 avocados and add to the bowl with the drained pasta. Drizzle over 4 tablespoons extra virgin olive oil and the juice of 2 limes. Season, toss to mix well and serve.

20 Corn and Courgette Cakes

Serves 4

150 g (5 oz) fresh sweetcorn
   kernels
1 courgette, coarsely grated
1 teaspoon cumin seeds
4 spring onions, thinly sliced
3 tablespoons self raising flour
2 eggs, beaten
2 tablespoons chopped
   fresh coriander
1 red chilli, deseeded and
   roughly chopped
vegetable oil, for shallow-frying
salt and pepper

To serve

ready-made guacamole
lime wedges

- Place the corn in a large bowl with the courgette, cumin seeds, spring onions, flour, eggs, coriander, chilli and some seasoning and mix well.

- Heat a tablespoon of oil in a large nonstick frying pan and cook spoonfuls of the mixture in batches for 2–3 minutes on each side until cooked through. You should end up with 12 cakes, 3 for each person.

- Serve with guacamole and lime wedges.

 Corn and Mixed Leaf Salad

Tip a 400 g (13 oz) can sweetcorn kernels into a salad bowl with a coarsely grated courgette and a 100 g (3½ oz) bag mixed salad leaves. Pour over 6 tablespoons ready-made Italian-Style vinaigrette, season, toss to mix well and serve.

 Creamy Courgette and Corn Pasta Bake

Cook 250 g (8 oz) dried rigatoni according to the packet instructions then drain and set aside in a large mixing bowl. Meanwhile, heat 2 tablespoons olive oil in a large frying pan and sauté 1 chopped onion and 2 chopped garlic cloves for 1–2 minutes. Add 1 finely diced courgette and 400 g (13 oz) fresh sweetcorn kernels and stir-fry for another minute or so. Mix 200 ml (7 fl oz) crème fraîche with 2 beaten eggs and a tablespoon Dijon mustard. Season well and add to the pasta with the vegetable mixture and 4 tablespoons chopped fresh coriander. Mix well, transfer to a shallow ovenproof dish and bake in a preheated oven, 200°C (400°F), Gas Mark 6, for 12–15 minutes. Remove from the oven and serve immediately.

30 Vegetable Spring Rolls

Serves 4

1 tablespoon groundnut oil

2 garlic cloves, finely chopped

small knob of fresh ginger, grated

1 red chilli, deseeded and
finely chopped

300 g (10 oz) bag mixed stir-fry
vegetables

1 tablespoon soy sauce

1 tablespoon rice wine vinegar

4 sheets filo pastry, each cut into
4 rectangles (about 15 x 12 cm/
6 x 5 in)

50 g (2 oz) salted butter, melted

sweet chilli sauce, to serve

- Heat a wok over a high heat and add the oil, garlic, ginger and chilli, then stir-fry for 30 seconds. Add the mixed vegetables, soy sauce and vinegar and cook for 1 minute. Spoon the vegetables into a sieve over a bowl and allow to cool slightly.

- Place a spoonful of the vegetable mixture in the centre of the narrow edge of a filo rectangle. Roll the filo around the mixture until halfway along the filo sheet, then fold each side of unfilled pastry into the centre. Continue rolling into a cylinder and brush with butter to seal. Repeat with the remaining pastry sheets.

- Place spring rolls on a baking tray and brush with butter. Bake in a preheated oven, 200°C (400°F), Gas Mark 6, for 12–15 minutes until golden and crisp. Serve hot with sweet chilli sauce.

 Vegetable Fried Rice

Heat 2 tablespoons vegetable oil in a large frying pan or wok over a high heat. Add 2 chopped garlic cloves, 1 teaspoon coarsely grated ginger, 500 g (1 lb) cooked white rice and a 300 g (10 oz) pack mixed stir-fry vegetables. Stir-fry over a high heat for 5–6 minutes or until piping hot. Stir in 6 tablespoons light soy sauce, 1 tablespoon sesame oil and 1 teaspoon chilli oil. Remove from the heat, stir in the juice of 1 lime and serve immediately.

 Thai Noodle and Vegetable Stir-Fry

Cover 250 g (8 oz) thin, rice noodles with boiling water in a large bowl. Cover and leave for 5 minutes and then drain. Meanwhile add 1 tablespoon vegetable oil to a large wok and place over a high heat. Add 2 teaspoons coarsely grated fresh root ginger, 2 chopped garlic cloves, 8 thinly sliced spring onions and 1 red chilli and stir-fry for 1 minute. Add a 300 g (10 oz) pack mixed stir-fry vegetables and cook for 3–4 minutes. Mix together 4 tablespoons each of sweet chilli sauce and hoisin sauce with 4 tablespoons water and tip into the wok. Stir-fry for another 3–4 minutes. Add the drained noodles along with 3 tablespoons each of chopped mint and coriander leaves and toss to mix well. Serve immediately in shallow bowls.

30 Devilled Eggs with Capers

Serves 4

6 eggs
1 teaspoon smoked paprika,
    plus extra to sprinkle
3 tablespoons mayonnaise
1 teaspoon English mustard
salt and pepper

To garnish

1 tablespoon small capers
1 tablespoon pink peppercorns,
    in brine, drained
thyme sprigs

- Place the eggs in a pan of salted water and bring to the boil. Cook until they are hard-boiled, about 10–15 minutes. Remove from the water and leave to cool.

- Shell the eggs and cut in half lengthwise.

- Scoop out the egg yolks and mash them together in a small mixing bowl. Mix in the paprika, mayonnaise and mustard and season well.

- Spoon the egg yolk mixture back into the egg white halves and garnish with the small capers, pink peppercorns and thyme sprigs. Sprinkle with paprika and serve.

 Chilli Fried Eggs with Warm Chapattis

Heat 2 tablespoons sunflower oil in a large frying pan over a medium heat. Carefully break 4 large eggs into the pan and fry for 2–3 minutes, or until cooked to your liking. Meanwhile, warm 4 chapattis in the microwave or warm oven. Place on to 4 warmed plates and top each chapatti with a fried egg. To serve, season and sprinkle over a mixture of 2 teaspoons dried chilli flakes, 1 teaspoon smoked paprika, 1 tablespoon small capers and 2 tablespoons finely chopped flat leaf parsley.

 Spicy Scrambled Eggs

Melt 2 tablespoons butter in a frying pan and fry 1 finely chopped onion and 3 chopped garlic cloves for 4–5 minutes, or until soft. Add 2 teaspoons cumin seeds, 1 teaspoon each of curry powder and ground turmeric and 1 chopped red chilli and cook for a further 4–5 minutes, or until fragrant and well combined. Add 2 finely chopped tomatoes and cook for a further 3–4 minutes more, or until softened. Beat 8 eggs with 100 ml (3½ fl oz) single cream in a bowl, then tip the mixture into the pan and cook, stirring constantly, until the eggs are just set. While the eggs are cooking, toast 4 large slices of sourdough bread and keep warm. Stir in 2 tablespoons finely chopped coriander, spoon the eggs on to the toast and serve immediately.

Substantial Soups and Salads

Recipes listed by cooking time

3⊘

2⊘

30 Spiced Potato, Coriander and Celeriac Soup

Serves 4

1 onion, chopped

2 tablespoons olive oil

1 garlic clove, chopped

½ teaspoons each of ground
  cumin and coriander

pinch of chilli flakes

2 small celeriac, peeled and
  finely diced

2 medium potatoes, peeled
  and finely diced

1 litre (1¾ pint) hot vegetable
  stock

25 g (1 oz) chopped coriander

4 tablespoons crème fraîche,
  to serve

toasted cumin seeds, to garnish

· Place the onion and olive oil in a pan with the garlic, ground cumin and coriander and a pinch of chilli flakes. Fry over a medium heat for 1 minute.

· Add the celeriac and potato, cover with the hot vegetable stock and bring to the boil. Simmer for 15–20 minutes or until the vegetables are tender.

· Stir in the chopped coriander and blend with a hand-held blender until fairly smooth.

· Serve in warmed bowls with a dollop of crème fraîche and toasted cumin seeds.

10 **Asian-style Celeriac, Carrot and Cabbage Slaw** In a large bowl mix together 1 coarsely grated celeriac, 2 coarsely grated carrots, ½ finely shredded red cabbage and a large handful of chopped coriander leaves. Mix 100 ml (3½ fl oz) crème fraîche together with 10 tablespoons mayonnaise, 1 teaspoon each of ground cumin, ground coriander and dried chilli flakes, and the juice of 2 limes. Season, pour over the celeriac mixture, toss to mix well and serve.

20 **Spicy Potato and Celeriac Stir-Fry** Heat 4 tablespoons vegetable oil in a large frying pan or wok and add 1 chopped onion, 1 chopped garlic clove, 1 teaspoon each of cumin and crushed coriander seeds and 1 chopped red chilli. Stir-fry over a medium heat for 2–3 minutes. Add 1 large coarsely grated potato and 1 large coarsely grated celeriac. Stir-fry over a high heat for 10–12 minutes or until the potato and celeriac are cooked through and tender. Remove from the heat and stir in a large handful of chopped coriander. Season and serve.

20 Beetroot and Apple Soup

Serves 4

1 tablespoon olive oil

1 tablespoon butter

2 Bramley apples, peeled, cored
and chopped

1 dessert apple, peeled, cored
and chopped

625 g (1¼ lb) cooked beetroot,
roughly chopped

2 teaspoons caraway seeds

4–5 fresh thyme sprigs

1.5 litres (2½ pints) vegetable stock

salt and pepper

crème fraîche, to serve

chopped dill, to garnish

- Heat the oil and butter in a pan and fry the apples for
2–3 minutes until golden. Add the cooked beetroot,
caraway seeds and thyme and stir-fry for 1–2 minutes.

- Add the stock, bring to the boil then cook for 10 minutes.

- In a blender or with a hand-held blender, whizz the soup
until fairly smooth and season to taste.

- Serve in bowls with crème fraîche swirled through. Garnish
with chopped dill and freshly ground black pepper.

10 Beetroot and Apple Salad

Thinly slice 6 large cooked
beetroot and place on a wide
salad platter with 4 cored and
sliced apples and the leaves of
2 heads of red chicory. Whisk
together 5 tablespoons olive
oil with 2 tablespoons cider
vinegar, 1 teaspoon clear honey,
1 teaspoon thyme leaves,
½ teaspoon caraway seeds and
1 teaspoon Dijon mustard. Season
and drizzle this dressing over the
salad. Toss to mix well and serve.

30 Beetroot and Apple Roast

Cut 6 large, cooked beetroot
into wedges and place in a
roasting tin with 6 peeled,
cored apples that have also been
cut into wedges. Drizzle over
4 tablespoons olive oil and add
4 thyme sprigs. Sprinkle over
2 teaspoons caraway seeds
and roast for 15–20 minutes.
Serve immediately over rice
or couscous.

30 Chunky Mushroom Soup

Serves 4

25 g (1 oz) butter
1 large onion, chopped
1 leek, finely sliced
2 garlic cloves, crushed
300 g (10 oz) chestnut
　mushrooms, roughly chopped
2 tablespoons plain flour
500 ml (17 fl oz) vegetable stock
400 ml (14 fl oz) milk
1 tablespoon finely chopped
　tarragon
salt and pepper
crusty bread, to serve

- Melt the butter in a pan over a low heat and gently sweat the onion, leek and garlic until they start to soften.

- Increase the heat and add the mushrooms to the pan, stirring until well combined. Continue to stir-fry for 2–3 minutes.

- Stir in the flour and continue to cook for 1 minute.

- Remove the pan from the heat and add the stock a little at a time, stirring well between each addition.

- Once all the stock is added, return the pan to the heat, bring to the boil, reduce the heat and simmer for a few minutes.

- Pour in the milk and bring to a simmer. Stir in the chopped tarragon and season to taste.

- Ladle the soup into bowls and serve with crusty bread.

10 **Mushroom Stir-Fry** Heat 2 tablespoons butter in a large wok and add 300 g (10 oz) sliced chestnut mushrooms, 2 chopped garlic cloves, 1 sliced onion and 1 sliced leek. Stir-fry over a high heat for 6–8 minutes, remove from the heat, stir in 4 tablespoons light soy sauce and serve over noodles or rice.

 20 **Mushroom, Leek and Tarragon Open Omelette** Heat 2 tablespoons butter in a large, nonstick frying pan and add 1 finely chopped leek, 2 chopped garlic cloves and 300 g (10 oz) finely chopped chestnut mushrooms. Stir-fry for 2–3 minutes and then pour in 6 beaten eggs. Season, sprinkle over 1 tablespoon chopped tarragon and cook for 6–8 minutes or until the base is just set; meanwhile, preheat the grill. Place the frying pan under a preheated hot grill for 3–4 minutes or until golden and puffed. Serve immediately with crusty bread and a salad.

20 Lettuce, Pea and Tarragon Soup

Serves 4

2 tablespoons butter

8 spring onions, trimmed
and sliced

750 g (1½ lb) frozen peas

1 tablespoon chopped
tarragon leaves

1 romaine lettuce, finely shredded

1 litre (1¾ pints) hot vegetable
stock

2 tablespoons double cream

salt and pepper

tarragon sprigs, to garnish
(optional)

- Melt the butter in a large saucepan over a medium heat. Add the spring onions and cook, stirring continuously, for 2 minutes.

- Stir in the peas, ½ of the tarragon and the lettuce. Cook for 1 minute.

- Add the stock, bring to the boil, cover and simmer for 5 minutes or until tender.

- Pour the soup into a blender, add the remaining tarragon and whizz until smooth. Season to taste.

- Divide the soup between 4 bowls, swirl the cream into each bowl and sprinkle with black pepper. Garnish with tarragon sprigs, if liked.

 Lettuce, Pea, Tomato and Spring Onion Salad Separate the leaves of 2 washed romaine lettuces and place in a large, wide salad bowl with 8 sliced spring onions, 4 sliced plum tomatoes, 500 g (1 lb) blanched peas and 12 sliced radishes. Make a dressing by whisking together the juice of 1 lemon, 6 tablespoons olive oil, 1 teaspoon Dijon mustard, 2 tablespoons finely chopped tarragon and 2 teaspoons clear honey. Season and pour over the salad ingredients. Toss to mix well and serve.

 Quinoa and Lettuce Taboulleh Put 200 g (7 oz) quinoa in a saucepan and dry-fry for 2–3 minutes. Add 600 ml (1 pint) hot vegetable stock, bring to the boil and stir to mix well. Reduce the heat and cook for 15–20 minutes or until all the liquid has been absorbed. Meanwhile, roughly chop the leaves of 1 romaine lettuce and add to a wide salad bowl with 6 finely chopped spring onions, 4 tablespoons each of finely chopped tarragon and parsley and 400 g (13 oz) blanched peas. Transfer the quinoa to the bowl and drizzle over 5 tablespoons olive oil and the juice of 1 orange. Season, toss to mix well and serve.

30 Hearty Minestrone

Serves 4

3 carrots, roughly chopped

1 red onion, roughly chopped

6 celery stalks, roughly chopped

2 tablespoons olive oil

2 garlic cloves, crushed

200 g (7 oz) potatoes, peeled
and cut into 1 cm (½ in) dice

4 tablespoons tomato purée

1.5 litres (2½ pints) vegetable
stock

400 g (13 oz) canned chopped
tomatoes

150 g (5 oz) short-shaped
soup pasta

400 g (13 oz) can cannellini beans,
drained

100 g (3½ oz) baby spinach

salt and pepper

- Whizz the carrots, onion and celery in a food processor until finely chopped.

- Heat the oil in a large saucepan, add the chopped vegetables, garlic, potatoes, tomato purée, stock, tomatoes and pasta. Bring to the boil, reduce the heat and simmer, covered, for 12–15 minutes.

- Tip in the cannellini beans and the spinach for the final 2 minutes of cooking time.

- Season to taste and serve with crusty bread.

10 Bean, Spinach and Pasta Salad

Drain a 400 g (13 oz) can cannellini beans and tip the beans into a large, wide bowl with 100 g (3½ oz) baby spinach, 2 coarsely grated carrots, ½ thinly sliced red onion and 200 g (7 oz) cooked short-shaped pasta. Pour over 6 tablespoons ready-made Italian-Style vinaigrette, toss to mix well and serve.

20 Chunky Pasta Sauce

Heat 2 tablespoons olive oil in a large frying pan and add 2 chopped garlic cloves, 1 chopped red onion, 2 chopped celery stalks, 1 chopped carrot and a 400 g (13 oz) can chopped tomatoes. Bring to the boil and simmer for 12–15 minutes. Meanwhile, cook 375 g (12 oz) short-shaped pasta according to the packet instructions.

Stir 100 g (3½ oz) baby spinach into the sauce with 200 g (7 oz) drained cannellini beans. Season well and serve over the cooked pasta with grated Parmesan.

20 Iced Green Gazpacho

Serves 4

2 celery stalks (including leaves)
1 small green pepper, deseeded
1 large cucumber, peeled
3 slices stale white bread,
    crusts removed
1 fresh green chilli, deseeded
4 garlic cloves
1 teaspoon clear honey
150 g (5 oz) walnuts, lightly toasted
200 g (7 oz) baby spinach
50 g (2 oz) basil leaves
4 tablespoons cider vinegar
250 ml (8 fl oz) extra virgin olive
    oil, plus extra for drizzling
6 tablespoons natural yogurt
475 ml (16 fl oz) iced water
handful of ice cubes
salt and pepper
ready-made croutons, to serve

- Roughly chop the celery, pepper, cucumber, bread, chilli and garlic.

- Place in a blender and add the honey, walnuts, spinach, basil, vinegar, oil, yogurt, most of the iced water and the ice cubes, and season well. Whizz the soup until smooth. Add more iced water, if needed, to achieve the desired consistency.

- Taste the soup and adjust the seasoning, if necessary.

- Serve in chilled bowls and garnish with croutons and a drizzle of olive oil.

---

10 Green Vegetable Salad

Place 4 finely sliced celery stalks, 1 sliced cucumber, 1 thinly sliced green pepper and 100 g (3½ oz) baby spinach into a large wide bowl. Make a dressing by whisking 150 ml (¼ pint) natural yogurt in a bowl with the juice 1 lime, 1 crushed garlic clove, 1 teaspoon clear honey and 1 finely diced green chilli. Drizzle over the salad and scatter over a small handful of ready-made croutons before serving.

30 Spiced Green Pilaf with Walnuts

Heat 3 tablespoons olive oil in a saucepan and add 4 crushed garlic cloves, 1 finely chopped green pepper, 2 chopped green chillis and 8 sliced spring onions. Stir-fry for 5–6 minutes. Stir in 200 g (7 oz) roughly chopped baby spinach and 2 teaspoons cumin seeds. Stir-fry for a further 3–4 minutes or until the spinach has wilted. Add 500 g (1 lb) cooked basmati rice, season well and stir-fry for 3–4 minutes or until piping hot. Serve immediately garnished with 100 g (3½ oz) chopped, toasted walnuts.

30 Jamaican Spiced Corn Chowder

Serves 4

1 tablespoon olive oil

1 large onion, finely chopped

2 garlic cloves, finely chopped

1 teaspoon cayenne pepper

200 g (7 oz) red split lentils, rinsed

1 litre (1¾ pints) hot vegetable
  stock

400 ml (14 fl oz) can coconut milk

1 Scotch bonnet chilli, left whole

1 tablespoon thyme leaves

200 g (7 oz) potatoes, peeled and
  cut into 1 cm (½ in) dice

200 g (7 oz) carrots, peeled and
  cut into 1 cm (½ in) dice

400 g (13 oz) sweetcorn kernels
  (either fresh, frozen or canned)

2 red peppers, cut into 1 cm
  (½ in) dice

salt and pepper

chopped coriander, to garnish

- Heat the oil in a saucepan and stir-fry the onion and garlic for 2–3 minutes.

- Increase the heat, add the cayenne pepper, red lentils, stock, coconut milk, chilli, thyme, potato and carrots. Bring to the boil and simmer for 15–20 minutes.

- Season and add the corn and red pepper for the last 3 minutes of cooking.

- Remove the Scotch bonnet chilli, ladle the chowder into warmed bowls and serve garnished with chopped coriander and sprinkled with freshly ground black pepper.

 Corn and Red Pepper Curry

Heat 1 tablespoon olive oil in a saucepan and fry 1 chopped onion and 2 chopped garlic cloves with 625 g (1¼ lb) sweetcorn kernels and 2 finely diced red peppers for 1–2 minutes. Add 1 tablespoon mild curry powder and 600 ml (1 pint) coconut milk and bring to the boil. Cook for 3–4 minutes, remove from the heat and stir in 4 tablespoons finely chopped fresh coriander before serving over rice.

 Spicy Corn Hash

Heat 1 tablespoon olive oil in a large frying pan. Add 1 chopped onion, 2 chopped garlic cloves, ¼ chopped Scotch bonnet chilli (you might want to wear washing-up gloves to do this as they're fiercely hot) and 1 teaspoon cayenne pepper. Stir-fry for 1–2 minutes and then add 200 g (7 oz) each coarsely grated potato and carrot, 500 g (1 lb) sweetcorn kernels and 1 finely diced red pepper. Add 200 ml (7 fl oz) coconut milk, stir and cook over a high heat for 10 minutes or until the liquid has evaporated and the vegetables are tender. Garnish with chopped fresh coriander before serving with crusty bread and a fried egg, if desired.

30 Oriental Rice Soup with Egg and Greens

Serves 4

4 spring onions
100 g (3½ oz) pak choi, roughly chopped
2 tablespoons vegetable oil
2.5 cm (1 in) piece root ginger, finely grated
2 garlic cloves, finely chopped
200 g (7 oz) jasmine rice
100 ml (3½ fl oz) rice wine
2 tablespoons soy sauce
1 teaspoon rice wine vinegar
1 litre (1¾ pints) hot vegetable stock
4 eggs
1 tablespoon chilli oil, for drizzling

- Finely slice the spring onions, keeping the white and green parts separate. Combine the green bits with the pak choi in a bowl and set aside.

- Heat the oil gently in a saucepan. When hot, add the onion whites, ginger and garlic and stir-fry for 2–3 minutes.

- Add the rice, stir, then add the wine and bubble for a minute or so.

- Add the soy sauce, vinegar and stock and simmer, stirring occasionally, for 10–12 minutes. Then stir in the reserved spring onions and pak choi and cook for a further 2–3 minutes. Meanwhile poach the eggs in two batches.

- To serve, ladle the soup into 4 shallow soup bowls and top each one with a poached egg and drizzle over the chilli oil.

 Oriental Rice and Asian Green Salad

Place 300 g (10 oz) blanched and roughly chopped pak choi in a salad bowl with 6 sliced spring onions and 500 g (1 lb) cooked jasmine rice. Make a dressing by whisking together 1 crushed garlic clove, 1 teaspoon grated ginger, ¼ teaspoon chilli oil, 2 tablespoons light soy sauce, the juice of 2 limes, a dash of rice wine vinegar and 4 tablespoons vegetable oil. Season, pour over the salad and toss to mix well before serving.

 Egg Noodle and Vegetable Stir-Fry

Heat 2 tablespoons vegetable oil in a large wok and add 8 sliced spring onions, 1 sliced red pepper, 2 chopped garlic cloves, 1 teaspoon finely chopped fresh root ginger. Stir-fry over a medium heat for 3–4 minutes. Add 400 g (13 oz) roughly chopped pak choi and stir-fry for a further 2–3 minutes. In a bowl mix together 1 tablespoon cornflour with 6 tablespoons light soy sauce, 100 ml (3½ fl oz) vegetable stock, 1 teaspoon chilli oil and 4 tablespoons rice wine vinegar. Pour into the wok, turn the heat to high and cook for 2–3 minutes. Add 400 g (13 oz) cooked fresh egg noodles, toss to mix well and heat until piping hot. Serve immediately.

30 Spinach and Red Lentil Soup

Serves 4

250 g (8 oz) dried red lentils
3 tablespoons sunflower oil
1 large onion, finely chopped
2 garlic cloves, crushed
2.5 cm (1 in) piece fresh root
  ginger, grated
1 red chilli, deseeded and chopped,
  plus extra to garnish (optional)
1 tablespoon medium curry powder
300 ml (½ pint) hot vegetable
  stock
200 g (7 oz) can tomatoes
100 g (3½ oz) baby leaf spinach
25 g (1 oz) chopped coriander
  leaves, plus extra to garnish
100 ml (3½ fl oz) coconut cream
salt and pepper
4 tablespoons natural yogurt,
  to serve

- Put the lentils into a medium saucepan and cover with 900 ml (1½ pints) cold water. Bring to the boil, skimming off the scum as it rises to the surface, and leave to simmer for 10 minutes until the lentils are tender and just falling apart. Remove from the heat, cover and set aside.

- Meanwhile, heat the oil in a large saucepan, add the onion and fry gently for 5 minutes. Add the garlic, ginger and chilli and fry for a further 2 minutes. Stir in the curry powder and ½ teaspoon black pepper and cook for a further 2 minutes.

- Add the stock, the lentils and their cooking liquid, the tomatoes, spinach and coriander and season with salt to taste. Cover and simmer for 5 minutes then add the coconut cream.

- Whizz the mixture with a hand-held blender, until the soup is almost smooth.

- Ladle the soup into 4 warmed bowls and garnish each with a spoonful of yogurt, the remaining coriander leaves, freshly ground black pepper and finely chopped red chilli, if desired.

10 Spinach, Green Lentil and Yellow Rice Pilaf

Heat 1 tablespoon oil in a large wok and add 1 chopped onion, 2 chopped garlic cloves, 1 teaspoon grated ginger, 1 chopped red chilli and 1 tablespoon curry powder. Stir-fry for 1–2 minutes and then add 2 x 250 g (8 oz) packs of cooked microwaveable pilau rice, 75 g (3 oz) chopped baby spinach and 100 ml (3½ fl oz) hot vegetable stock. Stir and cook over a high heat for 5–6 minutes or until piping hot. Tip in 200 g (7 oz) drained canned green lentils and stir. Cook until warmed through. Season and serve warm, with natural yogurt.

20 Spinach, Tomato and Coconut Curry

Heat 2 tablespoons oil in a pan and add 1 chopped onion, 2 chopped garlic cloves, 1 teaspoon grated ginger, 1 chopped red chilli and a tablespoon curry powder. Stir-fry for 1–2 minutes, then add 400 g (13 oz) chopped tomatoes, 200 ml (7 fl oz) coconut milk and 300 g (10 oz) spinach. Stir, season and cook over a medium heat for 10–12 minutes or until the spinach has wilted. Stir in a handful of chopped coriander leaves and serve with basmati rice.

Mixed Pulses and Baby Spinach Salad with Avocado Dressing

Serves 4

150 g (5 oz) baby spinach

1 large carrot, coarsely grated

150 g (5 oz) medium vine tomatoes, quartered

1 small red pepper, deseeded and thinly sliced

1 x 400 g (13 oz) can mixed beans, drained

100 g (3½ oz) can chickpeas, drained

2 tablespoons pumpkin seeds, lightly toasted

For the avocado dressing

1 ripe avocado

1 teaspoon Dijon mustard

juice of 1 lemon

1 teaspoon clear honey

dash of Tabasco sauce

4 tablespoons extra virgin olive oil

salt and pepper

- Mix the baby spinach leaves and carrot together and place onto a wide salad platter or into a large bowl.

- Add the tomatoes and pepper slices and scatter over the mixed beans, chickpeas and toasted pumpkin seeds.

- Halve the avocado and remove the stone. Scoop the flesh into a food processor and add the mustard, lemon juice, honey and Tabasco sauce. Blend until smooth then, with the motor still running, gradually pour in the oil and 2–3 tablespoons warm water. Season to taste.

- Drizzle the dressing over the salad and serve immediately.

 Rustic Mixed Bean and Spinach Soup

Heat 2 x 400 g (13 oz) cans of cream of tomato soup in a large saucepan and add a 400 g (13 oz) can of mixed beans (drained) and 200 g (7 oz) chopped baby spinach and bring to the boil. Simmer gently for 5–6 minutes, season and serve immediately.

 Individual Chickpea and Spinach Pots

Heat 2 tablespoons olive oil in a large frying pan and gently fry 1 chopped onion, ½ chopped red pepper and 1 crushed garlic clove until soft. Add 2 teaspoons cumin seeds, 2 teaspoons crushed coriander seeds and 1 teaspoon smoked paprika and cook for 1 minute. Add 400 g (13 oz) chopped vine tomatoes and 150 g (5 oz) chopped spinach along with 200 g (7 oz) each canned and drained chickpeas and mixed beans. Bring to the boil and simmer for 5 minutes. Whisk 200 ml (7 fl oz) natural yogurt and stir into the vegetable mixture. Season well and transfer to 4 deep individual pie or baking dishes. Sprinkle over 100 g (3½ oz) grated Cheddar cheese and bake in a preheated oven, 220°C (425°F), Gas Mark 7, for 10–15 minutes or until piping hot.

Tricolore Avocado and Couscous Salad

Serves 4

200 g (7 oz) couscous
300 ml (½ pint) hot vegetable
  stock or boiling water
250 g (8 oz) cherry tomatoes
2 avocados, peeled, stoned
  and chopped
150 g (5 oz) mozzarella cheese,
  drained and chopped
handful rocket leaves

For the dressing

2 tablespoons fresh green pesto
1 tablespoon lemon juice
4 tablespoons extra virgin olive oil
salt and pepper

- Mix the couscous and stock (or boiling water) together in a bowl then cover with a plate and leave for 10 minutes.

- To make the dressing, mix the pesto with the lemon juice and season, then gradually mix in the oil. Pour over the couscous and mix with a fork.

- Add the tomatoes, avocados and mozzarella to the couscous, mix well, then lightly stir in the rocket.

---

10 **Italian-Style Ciabatta with Cherry Tomatoes, Avocado and Mozzarella** Mix together 250 g (8 oz) chopped tomatoes, 2 chopped avocados, 200 g (7 oz) chopped mozzarella and season well. Halve and lighty toast 4 ciabatta rolls and spread with 8 tablespoons ready-made pesto. Divide the avocado mixture between the rolls, garnish with a few rocket leaves and serve.

30 **Cherry Tomato, Avocado and Mozzarella Pasta** Finely chop 300 g (10 oz) cherry tomatoes, 2 avocados, 50 g (2 oz) rocket and 200 g (7 oz) mozzarella cheese. Place in a bowl with 6 tablespoons ready-made pesto and 2 tablespoons olive oil. Season and stir to mix well. Allow to stand at room temperature for 15 minutes for the flavours to infuse. Meanwhile, cook 375 g (12 oz) spaghetti according to the packet instructions. Drain the pasta and transfer to a wide serving dish. Add the cherry tomato mixture, toss to mix well and serve.

30 Veggie Caesar-Style Salad with Garlic and Herb Croutons

Serves 4

2 red apples, cored and diced
4 celery stalks, thinly sliced
1 head of cos lettuce, leaves washed and roughly torn
4 spring onions, thinly sliced
bunch of chives, chopped
4 hard-boiled eggs, shelled and halved, to garnish

For the croutons

2 slices of crusty bread, cubed
2 teaspoons garlic salt
2 teaspoons dried mixed herbs
3 tablespoons olive oil

For the dressing

2 garlic cloves, crushed
2 tablespoons capers, drained
2 tablespoons lemon juice
2 teaspoons Dijon mustard
1 teaspoon sugar or clear honey
8 tablespoons grated Parmesan cheese
100 ml (3½ fl oz) natural yogurt
salt and pepper

- First make the croutons. Place the cubes of bread into a bowl and sprinkle over the garlic salt and dried herbs. Drizzle with the olive oil and toss to coat evenly.

- Place the croutons on a baking sheet in a single layer and bake in a preheated oven, 200°C (400°F), Gas Mark 6, for 10–12 minutes or until lightly browned and crisp. Remove from the oven and set aside.

- Meanwhile make the dressing. Place the garlic, capers, lemon juice, mustard, sugar or honey, Parmesan and yogurt in a blender and whizz till smooth. Season with black pepper. Chill until ready to use (you can make the dressing up to a day in advance, if desired).

- Place the apples, celery, lettuce, spring onions and chives in a wide salad bowl.

- Drizzle the dressing over the salad ingredients and toss to mix well.

- Garnish with the halved eggs and top with the garlic and herb croutons.

---

10 Crisp Lettuce Salad with Croutons

Place the leaves from 2 romaine or cos lettuces in a bowl with 6 sliced spring onions, 2 sliced celery stalks and 1 sliced cucumber. Drizzle over 8 tablespoons ready-made Caesar salad dressing, scatter over 100 g (3½ oz) ready-made croutons, season, toss to mix well and serve.

20 Caesar-Style Pasta Salad

Cook 200 g (7 oz) pennette or other short-shaped pasta according to the packet instructions. Meanwhile roughly chop the leaves of 1 cos or romaine lettuce, 6 spring onions, 2 celery stalks, a small handful of chopped chives and 4 chopped hard-boiled eggs, putting them all in a wide salad bowl. Drain the pasta and rinse under cold running water to cool, then drain and add to the salad mixture. Drizzle over 8 tablespoons ready-made Caesar salad dressing (or use from the recipe above), season, toss to mix well and serve.

Warm Pasta Salad with Lemon and Broccoli

Serves 4

375 g (12 oz) penne or rigatoni
150 g (5 oz) broccoli florets
100 g (3½ oz) frozen soya beans
100 g (3½ oz) frozen peas
100 g (3½ oz) sugarsnap peas,
  trimmed
150 g (5 oz) soft cheese with
  garlic and herbs
finely grated zest and juice
  of 1 lemon
4 tablespoons olive oil
1 red chilli, deseeded and finely
  chopped
100 g (3½ oz) grated pecorino
  cheese
2 tablespoons chopped tarragon
  leaves
salt and pepper

· Cook the pasta in a large saucepan following the pack instructions, adding the broccoli florets, soya beans, peas and sugarsnaps for the final 3 minutes of its cooking time.

· Drain the pasta and vegetables, saving a ladleful of the cooking water, then tip back into the pan.

· Stir in the soft cheese, lemon zest and juice, olive oil, chilli, pecorino, tarragon, some seasoning and a splash of cooking water.

· Serve the salad warm or at room temperature.

 Quick Broccoli and Vegetable Stir-Fry
Heat 2 tablespoons olive oil in a large wok. Add 300 g (10 oz) blanched broccoli florets, 100 g (3½ oz) soya beans, 100 g (3½ oz) peas, 100 g (3½ oz) sugarsnap peas, 2 crushed garlic cloves, 1 chopped red chilli and 1 teaspoon grated fresh root ginger. Stir-fry over a high heat for 4–5 minutes and then stir in a 100 g (3½ oz) sachet of ready-made stir-fry sauce of your choice. Stir-fry for 2–3 minutes and serve immediately over cooked noodles.

 Broccoli, Pasta and Mixed Pea Bake
Tip 500 g (1 lb) cooked rigatoni into a greased ovenproof dish with 150 g (5 oz) blanched broccoli florets, 100 g (3½ oz) peas, 100 g (3½ oz) soya beans and 100 g (3½ oz) blanched sugarsnap peas. Toss to mix well. In a separate bowl whisk together 3 eggs with 1 tablespoon finely grated lemon zest, 2 tablespoons finely chopped tarragon, 1 chopped red chilli and 150 g (5 oz) soft cheese with garlic and herbs. Season well. Pour the egg mixture into the ovenproof dish, sprinkle over 100 g (3½ oz) grated pecorino cheese and bake in a preheated oven, 220°C (425°F), Gas Mark 7, for 15–20 minutes or until the mixture is bubbling and lightly golden on the top. Serve hot or at room temperature.

30 Warm Moroccan Bulgar and Roasted Vegetable Salad

Serves 4

2 tablespoons harissa paste

2 tablespoons olive oil

500 g (1 lb) butternut squash and sweet potato, diced

2 red peppers, deseeded and cut into bite-sized pieces

125 g/4 oz bulgar wheat

600 ml (1 pint) hot vegetable stock

2 garlic cloves, crushed

juice of 1 lemon

200 ml (7 fl oz) natural yogurt

6 tablespoons each finely chopped coriander and mint leaves

salt and pepper

- Mix the harissa paste and oil together in a bowl and add the squash, sweet potato and red pepper and toss until well coated.

- Spread the vegetables on a large baking tray and roast in a preheated oven, 200°C (400°F), Gas Mark 6, for 20 minutes until softened and the edges of the vegetables are starting to char.

- Meanwhile put the bulgar wheat in a large bowl and pour over the hot stock, then cover and leave to absorb the liquid for 15 minutes until the grains are tender, but still have a little bite.

- In a separate bowl, mix the garlic and lemon juice into the yogurt and season to taste.

- Leave the bulgar wheat to cool slightly then toss in the roasted vegetables, chopped coriander and mint. Serve warm with the yogurt mixture.

 Superfast Harissa and Roasted Veg Soup Place the roasted vegetables from the recipe above in a blender with 500 ml (17 fl oz) hot vegetable stock, 1 tablespoon harissa paste and 3 tablespoons each of chopped coriander and mint. Blend until smooth and serve in warmed bowls with a dollop of natural yogurt.

 Middle Eastern Butternut and Sweet Potato Stew Heat 2 tablespoons oil in a saucepan and add 1 chopped onion, 2 chopped garlic cloves, 2 finely chopped red peppers and 400 g (13 oz) finely diced butternut squash and sweet potato. Stir-fry for 1–2 minutes. Add 500 ml (17 fl oz) hot vegetable stock and 1 tablespoon harissa paste and bring to the boil. Cook for 10–15 minutes or until the vegetables are tender. Season and stir in 2 tablespoons each of finely chopped coriander and mint leaves. Serve with cooked bulgar wheat or couscous.

# Quails' Egg Salad with Baby Spinach Leaves

Serves 4

100 g (3½ oz) baby spinach
1 red onion, sliced
200 g (7 oz) yellow and red
 cherry tomatoes, halved
1 tablespoon wholegrain mustard
6 tablespoons avocado oil
juice of 1 lemon
1 teaspoon clear honey
12 quails' eggs, hard-boiled
 and shelled
salt and pepper

- Place the spinach, red onion, tomatoes in a wide mixing bowl.

- In another bowl, mix together the mustard, oil, lemon juice and honey. Season well and stir until well combined.

- Divide the salad between 4 serving plates.

- Halve 4 of the eggs, leaving the rest whole, and scatter over the salad, drizzling the dressing over each serving.

 Ciabatta with Quails' Eggs and Salad Split 4 warmed, individual ciabattas and spread each base with 2 tablespoons mayonnaise and 1 tablespoon wholegrain mustard. Mix together 1 sliced red onion, a small handful of baby spinach and 100 g (3½ oz) sliced cherry tomatoes. Spoon this mixture over the ciabatta bases. Top with 12 halved hard-boiled quails' eggs. Replace the lids and serve.

 Warm Quails' Egg and Rice Salad Cook 200 g (7 oz) easy-cook rice according to the packet instructions. Meanwhile, place 100 g (3½ oz) baby spinach in a wide salad bowl with 1 finely chopped red onion, 400 g (13 oz) halved red and yellow cherry tomatoes and 12 hard-boiled and shelled quails' eggs. Make a dressing by whisking together 6 tablespoons avocado oil with the juice of 1 lemon, 1 teaspoon clear honey and 1 tablespoon wholegrain mustard and season well. Pour over the salad ingredients with the warm, cooked rice and a small handful of chopped flat leaf parsley. Toss to mix well and serve.

Watermelon, Olive, Green Bean and Feta Salad

Serves 4

300 g (10 oz) green beans, halved

1 red onion

juice of 2 limes

1.5 kg (3 lb) watermelon, ripe and sweet

250 g (8 oz) feta cheese

100 g (3½ oz) black olives, pitted

1 bunch flat leaf parsley, roughly chopped

1 bunch mint leaves, roughly chopped

5 tablespoons extra virgin olive oil

salt and pepper

- Blanch the green beans in a saucepan of boiling water for 3 minutes. Drain, refresh under cold water and set aside.

- Halve the red onion and cut into thin slices. Place in a small bowl with the drained beans and the lime juice and allow to steep. Season with salt.

- Remove the rind and pips from the watermelon and cut into bite-sized pieces. Cut the feta into similarly sized pieces and put them both into a large, wide, shallow bowl or serving dish.

- Add the red onions and beans, along with their juices, to the wide bowl or serving dish. Scatter over the olives and herbs.

- Season well, drizzle with oil and serve at room temperature.

 Moroccan Orange and Black Olive Salad with Feta Peel and segment 4 large oranges (saving any juices) and place them on a serving platter with 100 g (3½ oz) pitted black olives and 250 g (8 oz) cubed feta cheese. Drizzle over 4 tablespoons olive oil and sprinkle over 2 teaspoons of Moroccan spice mix. Season, toss to mix well and scatter over a small handful of mint leaves to serve.

 Quinoa Salad with Olives, Green Beans and Feta Cook the quinoa according to the packet instructions, allow to cool and transfer it to a wide bowl. Meanwhile, quarter 3 red onions, drizzle over 1 tablespoon olive oil and roast in a preheated oven, 220°C (425°F), Gas Mark 7, for 12–15 minutes. Blanch 625 g (1¼ lb) halved green beans in a saucepan of boiling water for 3 minutes. Drain, refresh under cold water and add to the quinoa. Add the roasted red onion, a handful each of finely chopped mint and parsley, 100 g (3½ oz) green olives and 200 g (7 oz) feta cheese. Season, drizzle over the juice of 1 orange and 5 tablespoons olive oil. Toss to mix well and serve.

10 Delicatessen Pasta Salad

Serves 4

2 x 300 g (10 oz) packs fresh
spinach and ricotta tortellini

1 x 275 g (9 oz) jar mixed sliced
roasted peppers in olive oil

1 x 275 g (9 oz) jar mushrooms
in olive oil, drained

200 g (7 oz) Sunblush tomatoes,
drained

25 g (1 oz) basil leaves

50 g (2 oz) rocket leaves

black pepper

- Bring a large pan of lightly salted water to the boil. Add the tortellini and cook according to the pack instructions. Drain well and tip into a large bowl.

- Add the jar of mixed peppers, including the oil, along with the drained mushrooms and Sunblush tomatoes.

- Add the basil leaves and rocket. Season with black pepper, stir gently to combine and serve warm.

---

2 Italian-Style Pasta Broth

Bring 1 litre (1¾ pint) vegetable stock to the boil in a large saucepan and add 1 diced carrot, 1 diced onion and 1 diced celery stalk. Bring back to the boil and cook for 10 minutes. Add 2 x 300 g (10 oz) packs of fresh spinach and ricotta tortellini and cook for 3–4 minutes. Remove from the heat and stir in 25 g (1 oz) each of chopped basil and chopped rocket leaves and serve ladled into warmed bowls.

3 Tortellini Pasta Bake

Cook 2 x 300 g (10 oz) packs fresh spinach and ricotta tortellini, drain and mix together in a shallow ovenproof dish with 200 g (7 oz) roasted mixed peppers, 200 g (7 oz) Sunblush tomatoes and 25 g (1 oz) chopped basil leaves. Whisk together 2 eggs, 200 ml (7 fl oz) double cream and 50 g (2 oz) grated Parmesan cheese. Season and pour over the tortellini mixture. Bake in a preheated oven, 200°C (400°F), Gas Mark 6, for 15–20 minutes or until bubbling and golden. Serve warm with a rocket salad.

20 Fatoush Salad

Serves 4

1 pitta bread, torn into
  small pieces
6 plum tomatoes, deseeded
  and roughly chopped
½ cucumber, peeled and
  roughly chopped
10 radishes, sliced
1 red onion, roughly chopped
1 small little gem lettuce,
  leaves separated
small handful of fresh mint leaves

For the dressing

200 ml (7 fl oz) olive oil
juice of 3 lemons
1 garlic clove, crushed
2 teaspoons sumac (or
  ½ teaspoons ground cumin)
salt and pepper

- First make the dressing. Whisk the olive oil, lemon juice, garlic and sumac together in a bowl. Season to taste.

- To make the salad, combine the pitta pieces, tomatoes, cucumber, radishes, red onion, lettuce leaves and mint leaves in a large bowl.

- When ready to serve, pour the dressing over the salad and gently mix together to coat the salad evenly.

---

10 Middle Eastern Couscous Salad

Replace the pitta bread in the above recipe with 400 g (13 oz) cooked couscous. Pour over the dressing, toss to mix well and serve.

30 Toasted Pitta, Hummus and Salad

'Pizzettas' Finely dice 4 plum tomatoes, ½ cucumber, 6 radishes, ½ red onion and place in a bowl with 1 crushed garlic clove, 4 tablespoons olive oil, 2 teaspoons sumac and the juice of 1 lemon. Season and stir to mix well. Allow to stand for 15 minutes. Meanwhile, toast 8 pitta breads until lightly golden and place on to 4 serving plates. Spread 2 tablespoons hummus over each one and then top with the prepared salad. Sprinkle over chopped mint leaves and serve.

30 Fruity Potato Salad

Serves 4

300 g (10 oz) new potatoes, scrubbed

2 oranges, segmented

2 red dessert apples, cored and roughly chopped

100 g (3½ oz) green and red seedless grapes

2 celery stalks, thickly sliced

6 spring onions, sliced

4 large gherkins, roughly chopped

For the dressing

6 tablespoons mayonnaise

juice of 1 lemon

1 teaspoon clear honey

1 tablespoon wholegrain mustard

3 tablespoons each of finely chopped dill and chives

salt and pepper

- First make the dressing. Mix together all the ingredients in a bowl and season to taste.

- Cook the potatoes in boiling salted water for about 15–20 minutes until just tender. Drain and, when just cool enough to handle, cut into halves or quarters if quite large.

- Place the potatoes in a mixing bowl with the remaining salad ingredients. Pour on the dressing and toss gently to mix well. Chill the salad until ready to serve.

1 **Fruity Pasta Salad** Replace the potatoes in above recipe with 200 g (7 oz) quick-cook penne pasta and cook according to the packet instructions. Place in a bowl with the oranges, apples, grapes, celery and spring onions. Pour over the dressing, toss to mix well and serve.

2 **Mustardy Potato and Spring Onion Gratin** Place 625 g (1¼ lb) cooked, sliced new potatoes in a lightly oiled gratin or shallow ovenproof dish. Add 6 finely sliced spring onions, 2 finely sliced celery stalks and 2 finely chopped gherkins. Toss to mix well. Whisk together 10 tablespoons fresh mayonnaise with 2 tablespoons wholegrain mustard, 3 tablespoons each of chopped dill and chives and 1 egg. Spoon this over the vegetables and place under a preheated medium-hot grill for 4–5 minutes or until golden and bubbling. Serve immediately.

10 Kachumber and Basmati Rice Salad

Serves 4

1 red onion, finely chopped

6 ripe tomatoes, finely chopped

1 cucumber, finely chopped

1 fresh red chilli, deseeded and
finely chopped

small handful of finely chopped
coriander

small handful of finely chopped
mint

400 g (13 oz) basmati rice,
cooked and cooled

juice of 2 large limes

2 tablespoons roughly chopped
roasted peanuts

salt and pepper

- Put the onion, tomatoes, cucumber, chilli, coriander, mint
and rice in a bowl, and pour over the lime juice.

- Season well, cover and allow to stand at room temperature
for 5–6 minutes.

- Before serving, stir to mix well and sprinkle over the
chopped nuts.

20 Linguini with a Fresh Tomato, Chilli and Herb Sauce

Cook 375 g (12 oz) linguini
according to the packet
instructions. Meanwhile finely
chop 1 red onion, 6 plum
tomatoes, 1 red chilli and a
small handful coriander and
mint leaves. Place in a bowl
with 6 tablespoons olive oil,
season and stir to mix well.
When the pasta is cooked, drain
and divide between 4 serving
plates. Top with the pasta sauce
and serve immediately.

30 Cheesy Rice and Chilli

Vegetable Bake Place
1 chopped red onion, 6 chopped
tomatoes, 1 chopped red chilli
and 250 g (8 oz) cooked basmati
rice in a lightly oiled ovenproof
dish. Lightly beat 4 eggs in a
bowl with 1 teaspoon each of
grated fresh root ginger and
garlic, 3 tablespoons each of
finely chopped coriander and
mint and then season well. Pour
the egg mixture into the dish,
sprinkle over 200 g (7 oz)
grated Cheddar cheese and
bake in a preheated oven,
200 °C (400 °F), Gas Mark 6,
for 20–25 minutes or until just
set and golden. Serve with a
crisp green salad.

Couscous Salad With Peppers and Preserved Lemon

Serves 4

200 g (7 oz) giant couscous

750 ml (1½ pint) hot vegetable stock

2 garlic cloves, crushed

½ teaspoon finely grated fresh root ginger

1 teaspoon ground cumin

¼ teaspoon ground cinnamon

1 tablespoon orange zest

100 g (3½ oz) pumpkin seeds

4 tablespoons olive oil

1 red pepper and 1 yellow pepper, deseeded and finely chopped

4 spring onions, finely sliced

100 g (3½ oz) cherry tomatoes, quartered

1 tablespoon preserved lemon, drained and finely chopped

juice of 1 large orange

2 tablespoons each finely chopped coriander and mint leaves

- Place the couscous in a saucepan with the stock, garlic, ginger, cumin, cinnamon and orange zest. Bring to the boil and simmer for 10–12 minutes or until the couscous is tender.

- Meanwhile, toast the pumpkin seeds in a dry frying pan.

- Drain the couscous and place in a large mixing bowl with the olive oil, peppers, spring onions, tomatoes and preserved lemon.

- Add the orange juice, chopped herbs and pumpkin seeds. Toss gently to mix well and serve immediately.

---

10 **Vegetable and Giant Couscous Broth** Finely dice 1 red pepper and 1 yellow pepper and add to a saucepan with 4 sliced spring onions, 1 crushed garlic clove and 1. 2 litres (2 pints) hot vegetable stock. Bring to the boil and cook over a vigorous heat for 6–7 minutes. Stir in 100 g (3½ oz) cooked giant couscous and 2 tablespoons each of chopped coriander and mint leaves. Season and serve immediately.

30 **Mixed Pepper Tagine** Heat 3 tablespoons olive oil in a saucepan and add 4 chopped spring onions, 2 chopped garlic cloves, 1 teaspoon grated fresh root ginger, 1 teaspoon ground cumin, ¼ teaspoon ground cinnamon and 2 deseeded and chopped peppers (1 red and 1 yellow). Stir-fry for 2–3 minutes and then pour over 500 ml (17 fl oz) hot vegetable stock. Bring to the boil and simmer for 10–12 minutes and then add 1 tablespoon chopped preserved lemon. Mix together 1 tablespoon cornflour with 2 tablespoons cold water, add to the tagine, stir and cook until thickened slightly. Remove from the heat and garnish with chopped coriander before serving with couscous or rice.

20 Lentil, Mushroom and Peppadew Pepper Salad

Serves 4

4 tablespoons olive oil
300 g (10 oz) button mushrooms, halved or quartered
2 tablespoons cider vinegar
1 tablespoon Dijon mustard
200 g (7 oz) mild Peppadew peppers, drained and roughly chopped
6 spring onions, finely sliced
1 x 400 g (13 oz) can green lentils, drained and rinsed
3 little gem lettuces, leaves separated
100 g (3½ oz) goats' cheese
black pepper

· Heat 2 tablespoons of the oil in a nonstick frying pan. Add the mushrooms and fry over a high heat until just starting to soften.

· Remove from the heat, then stir in the remaining oil with the vinegar and mustard. Stir well until mixed, then add the Peppadew peppers, spring onion and lentils and mix well again.

· Arrange the salad leaves over 4 plates. Spoon the lentil salad over the top, crumble over the goats' cheese and serve sprinkled with freshly ground black pepper.

---

10 Lentil and Mushroom Pilaf

Heat 3 tablespoons olive oil in a frying pan over a high heat. Add 6 chopped spring onions and 300 g (10 oz) sliced mushrooms and stir-fry for 2–3 minutes. Add 500 g (1 lb) cooked basmati rice, 4 tablespoons chopped Peppadew peppers and 200 g (7 oz) canned, drained green lentils and stir-fry for 3–4 minutes or until piping hot. Remove from the heat and crumble over 100 g (3½ oz) goats' cheese before serving.

30 Spiced Mushroom and Lentil Curry

Heat 2 tablespoons olive oil in a saucepan and fry 6 chopped spring onions, 2 chopped garlic cloves and 1 teaspoon finely chopped fresh root ginger for 2–3 minutes over a low heat. Add 2 teaspoons cumin seeds, 1 teaspoon black mustard seeds and 2 tablespoons mild curry powder and stir-fry for 1–2 minutes. Stir in 400 g (13 oz) sliced button mushrooms and stir-fry over a high heat for 3–4 minutes. Add 400 g (13 oz) canned green lentils, 200 g (7 oz) chopped tomatoes and 200 ml (7 fl oz) vegetable stock. Bring to the boil and simmer gently for 15–20 minutes. Remove from the heat, stir in 4 tablespoons crème fraîche, season and serve with rice or warmed naan breads.

30 Insalata Russa or Russian Salad

Serves 4

2 or 3 waxy potatoes
2 cooked medium beetroot
100 g (3½ oz) fresh shelled peas
100 g (3½ oz) baby carrots
½ small cauliflower, broken into
   small florets
100 g (3½ oz) green beans, sliced
3 large eggs, hard-boiled
6 pickled gherkins with dill, finely
   chopped
6 tablespoons mayonnaise
salt and pepper
small bunch of fresh dill,
   to garnish

- Peel the potatoes and chop into 1 cm (½ in) cubes. Boil in a pan of lightly salted water for 10–12 minutes or until tender.

- Chop the beetroot into cubes roughly the same size as the potatoes and place in a wide salad bowl.

- Meanwhile blanch the peas, carrots, cauliflower and beans for 3–4 minutes. Drain and cool.

- Shell and halve the eggs.

- Mix the gherkins with the vegetables and then fold the mixture into the mayonnaise in a large bowl. Season and top with the eggs and a few dill sprigs.

1 Rainbow Vegetable Sauté

Heat 3 tablespoons olive oil in a large frying pan and add 1 chopped onion, 300 g (10 oz) each of cooked, diced beetroot, potatoes and carrots, 200 g (7 oz) peas and 300 g (10 oz) trimmed green beans. Stir-fry over a high heat for 6–7 minutes, season well and remove from the heat. Serve with rice or crusty bread.

2 Creamy Mixed Vegetable Soup

Place 100 g (3½ oz) each of finely diced cooked beetroot, potatoes and carrots in a saucepan with 200 g (7 oz) peas and 200 g (7 oz) roughly chopped green beans. Add 750 ml (1¼ pints) hot vegetable stock and bring to the boil. Cook over a high heat for 10 minutes and then stir in 200 ml (7 fl oz) single cream and 4 tablespoons finely chopped dill. Season, remove from the heat and serve.

Grilled Haloumi, Mixed Peppers and Rocket Salad

Serves 4

24 vine-ripened cherry tomatoes

200 g (7 oz) mixed peppers in olive oil (from a jar), drained and sliced

100 g (3½ oz) rocket leaves

2 x 200 g (7 oz) packs haloumi, sliced

For the dressing

grated zest of ½ lemon and 2 tablespoons juice

5 tablespoons olive oil

a handful flat leaf parsley, chopped

2 tablespoons small capers, drained and rinsed

black pepper

- First make the dressing. Whisk together the lemon zest and juice, olive oil, parsley, capers and black pepper, then set aside.

- Halve the tomatoes and divide among 4 plates, along with the peppers and rocket.

- Place the slices of haloumi on a preheated griddle pan and place under a preheated medium grill. Cook for 2–3 minutes on each side until just beginning to warm and soften.

- Transfer the warm haloumi to the plates, drizzle with the dressing and serve immediately.

 **Mediterranean Grilled Haloumi Wraps** In a large bowl, mix together 2 tablespoons capers, 300 g (10 oz) halved cherry tomatoes, 200 g (7 oz) chopped roasted mixed peppers (from a jar) and 40 g (1½ oz) chopped rocket leaves. Squeeze over the juice of 1 lime and season well. Meanwhile, warm 200 g (7 oz) sliced haloumi and 4 large flat-bread wraps in a preheated oven, 150°C (300°F), Gas Mark 2. To serve, divide the vegetable mixture and haloumi between the 4 wraps and fold over to enclose the filling.

 Pasta with Haloumi, Rocket and Cherry Tomatoes Cut 300 g (10 oz) haloumi into small bite-sized cubes. Heat 4 tablespoons olive oil in a large frying pan. Add the haloumi and stir-fry until lightly golden. Remove from the pan with a slotted spoon and set aside. Add 2 crushed garlic cloves to the pan and sauté for 1 minute. Add 300 g (10 oz) halved cherry tomatoes and 1 finely chopped red chilli and cook over a low heat for about 10 minutes until soft. Meanwhile cook 375 g (12 oz) short-shaped pasta according to the packet instructions, adding 50 g (2 oz) rocket leaves during the last minute of cooking. Drain the pasta and add to the cherry tomato mixture in the pan. Toss to mix well. Top with the drained haloumi, season and serve.

20 Quinoa, Courgette and Pomegranate Salad

Serves 4

75 g (3 oz) quinoa
1 large courgette
1 tablespoon white wine vinegar
4 tablespoons olive oil
4 spring onions, finely sliced
100 g (3½ oz) cherry tomatoes, halved
1 red chilli, finely chopped
100 g (3½ oz) pomegranate seeds (or seeds of ½ pomegranate)
small handful of finely chopped flat leaf parsley
salt and pepper

- Cook the quinoa following the packet instructions then drain and rinse under cold water. Drain again.

- Cut the ends off the courgette then cut into ribbons using a potato peeler.

- Whisk together the vinegar and 2 tablespoons of the oil and season with salt and pepper.

- Put the rest of the ingredients in a large bowl, then pour over the dressing and toss everything together and serve.

---

10 Courgette and Spring Onion Stir-Fry Heat 2 tablespoons olive oil in a large wok and add 2 coarsely grated courgettes, 6 sliced spring onions and 100 g (3½ oz) roughly chopped cherry tomatoes. Stir-fry over a high heat for 3–4 minutes. Add a 100 g (3½ oz) sachet of a favourite ready-made stir-fry sauce and stir-fry for 2–3 minutes until piping hot. Serve with noodles or rice.

30 Warm Grilled Courgette and Aubergine Salad with Quinoa Cook 50 g (2 oz) quinoa according to the packet instructions. Meanwhile, slice 2 large courgettes, and 1 aubergine into 1 cm (½ in) slices, brush with a little olive oil and cook in a griddle pan over a high heat in batches for 4–5 minutes on each side or until tender. Place in a wide bowl and scatter over 4 finely sliced spring onions, 100 g (3½ oz) halved cherry tomatoes and the cooked quinoa. Drizzle with a mixture of 4 tablespoons olive oil and 1 tablespoon white wine vinegar. Season, scatter with mint leaves and serve.

Speedy Midweek Meals

Recipes listed by cooking time

30

2

20 Quick Roasted Vegetable Pizzas

Serves 4

2 ready-made chilled pizza dough
  bases (each about 23 cm/9 in
  in diameter)
400 g (13 oz) ready-made
  tomato pizza sauce
16–20 black olives, pitted
400 g (13 oz) roasted mixed
  peppers in olive oil (from a jar),
  drained and roughly chopped
200 g (7 oz) Sunblush tomatoes
3 tablespoons caperberries
8 chargrilled artichoke hearts in
  oil, drained and quartered
250 g (8 oz) mozzarella cheese,
  diced
roughly chopped parsley or
  oregano leaves, to garnish

- Preheat the oven to 220°C (425°F), Gas Mark 7.

- Place the pizza bases on 2 baking sheets.

- Spread the pizza sauce evenly over the pizza bases
  and scatter over the olives, roasted peppers, Sunblush
  tomatoes, caperberries, artichoke hearts and mozzarella.

- Bake in the preheated oven for 12–15 minutes until golden
  and crispy.

- Remove from the oven and garnish with the chopped herbs
  before serving.

---

10 Mediterranean Roasted Pepper

Salad Place 625 g (1¼ lb) roasted red and yellow peppers (from a jar), drained, in a wide bowl with 25 pitted black olives, 200 g (7 oz) Sunblush tomatoes, 4 tablespoons caperberries, 8 quartered chargrilled artichoke hearts and 250 g (8 oz) sliced mozzarella cheese. Toss in a handful of rocket leaves, drizzle with 4 tablespoons of olive oil and the juice of 1 lemon. Season, toss to mix well and serve.

30 Warm Mediterranean

Rice Salad Place 250 g (8 oz) long-grain rice in a heavy-based saucepan with 500 ml (17 fl oz) vegetable stock. Bring to the boil, cover and reduce the heat. Cook gently for 15 minutes and then turn the heat off and allow to stand undisturbed for another 10–15 minutes. Meanwhile, place 200 g (7 oz) roasted red and yellow peppers (from a jar), drained, in a wide bowl with 25 g (1 oz) pitted black

olives, 200 g (7 oz) Sunblush tomatoes, 4 tablespoons caperberries and 250 g (8 oz) diced mozzarella. Fluff up the grains of rice with a fork and fold into the vegetables with a small handful of chopped basil leaves. Season, toss to mix well and serve warm.

30 Black-Eyed Bean and Red Pepper 'Stew'

Serves 4

2 tablespoons olive oil

4 shallots, finely chopped

2 garlic cloves, crushed

2 celery stalks, diced

1 large carrot, peeled and cut into 1 cm (½ in) pieces

1 red pepper, deseeded and cut into 1 cm (½ in) pieces

1 teaspoon dried mixed herbs

2 teaspoons ground cumin

1 teaspoon ground cinnamon

2 x 400 g (13 oz) cans tomatoes

2 tablespoons sun-dried tomato purée

75 ml (3 fl oz) vegetable stock

2 x 400 g (13 oz) cans black-eyed beans in water, drained

4 tablespoons finely chopped coriander leaves, plus extra to garnish

salt and pepper

cooked basmati rice, to serve

- Heat the oil in a large frying pan and place over a high heat.

- Add the shallots, garlic, celery, carrot and red pepper and stir-fry for 2–3 minutes or until lightly starting to brown.

- Add the dried herbs, cumin, cinnamon, tomatoes, tomato purée and stock and bring to the boil. Reduce the heat to medium, cover and cook gently for 12–15 minutes or until the vegetables are tender, breaking up the tomatoes into small pieces with a wooden spoon towards the end of the cooking time.

- Stir in the black-eyed beans and cook for 2–3 minutes or until piping hot.

- Season well, remove from the heat and sprinkle over the chopped coriander. Garnish with coriander leaves and serve with basmati rice.

---

10 **Colourful Black-Eyed Bean and Vegetable Salad** Finely chop 2 carrots, 2 celery stalks, 1 red pepper, 2 tomatoes and 2 shallots and place in a bowl with 4 tablespoons olive oil and the juice of 2 limes. Season and add 1 x 400 g (13 oz) can black-eyed beans, drained, and a large handful of chopped coriander and mint leaves. Toss to mix well and serve with warm flatbreads.

20 **Hearty Bean and Vegetable Broth** Place 1 finely diced carrot, 2 finely diced celery stalks, 2 finely diced shallots, 2 crushed garlic cloves, 2 tablespoons sun-dried tomato purée and 2 teaspoons dried mixed herbs in a heavy-based saucepan with 1 litre (1¾ pints) hot vegetable stock and bring to the boil. Cook, uncovered, over a medium heat for 10–12 minutes. Stir in 2 x

400 g (13 oz) cans black-eyed beans, drained, and bring back to the boil. Season, remove from the heat and serve ladled into warmed bowls with crusty bread.

30 Creamy Courgette Orzo Pasta

Serves 4

375 g (12 oz) dried orzo (rice-shaped pasta)

1 tablespoon butter

1 tablespoon olive oil

1 red chilli, deseeded and finely chopped

2 garlic cloves, finely chopped

4 spring onions, very finely chopped

3 medium courgettes, coarsely grated

finely grated zest of 1 small unwaxed lemon

150 g (5 oz) soft cheese with garlic and herbs

4 tablespoons finely chopped flat leaf parsley

salt and pepper

- Bring a large pan of lightly salted water to the boil, then cook the pasta according to the packet instructions.

- Meanwhile, heat the butter and olive oil in a large frying pan, then add the chilli, garlic, spring onions and courgettes. Cook over a medium-low heat for 10–15 minutes, or until softened, stirring often.

- Reduce the heat and add the lemon zest. Cook gently for 3–4 minutes, add the soft cheese and mix thoroughly. Season to taste.

- Drain the pasta and add to the courgette mixture. Stir in the parsley, mix well and serve immediately.

10 Stir-Fried Courgettes with Spring Onion and Chilli

Heat 2 tablespoons olive oil in a large frying pan. Add 6 sliced spring onions, 2 crushed garlic cloves, 1 chopped red chilli and 3 coarsely grated courgettes. Stir-fry over a high heat for 4–5 minutes and then add 2 x 300 g (10 oz) packs fresh stir-fry rice noodles and 4 tablespoons light soy sauce. Toss to mix well and stir-fry for 2–3 minutes or until piping hot. Serve immediately.

20 Minted Courgette, Cherry Tomato and Orzo Pasta Salad

Cook 375 g (12 oz) orzo pasta according to the packet instructions. Meanwhile, place 2 coarsely grated courgettes, 4 sliced spring onions, 4 tablespoons finely chopped mint leaves and 200 g (7 oz) halved cherry tomatoes in a wide salad bowl. Make a dressing by whisking together 1 finely chopped red chilli, 2 crushed garlic cloves, 6 tablespoons olive oil, the juice of 1 lemon and 1 teaspoon honey. Season well. Drain the pasta and rinse under cold running water until cool. Drain again and add to the salad bowl. Pour over the dressing and toss to mix well before serving.

30 Greek-Style Summer Omelette

Serves 4

8 large eggs
1 teaspoon dried oregano
1 tablespoon finely chopped mint
4 tablespoons finely chopped
   flat leaf parsley
2 tablespoons olive oil
2 small red onions, peeled and
   roughly chopped
2 large ripe tomatoes, roughly
   chopped
½ courgette, roughly chopped
100 g (3½ oz) black olives, pitted
100 g (3½ oz) feta cheese
salt and pepper
crisp green salad, to serve
   (optional)

- Whisk the eggs in a bowl and add the oregano, mint and parsley. Season well.

- Heat the oil in a large nonstick frying pan. Add the red onion and fry over a high heat for about 3–4 minutes or until brown around the edges.

- Add the tomatoes, courgette and olives and cook for 3–4 minutes or until the vegetables begin to soften.

- Meanwhile, preheat the grill to medium-high.

- Reduce the heat to medium and pour the eggs into the frying pan. Cook for 3–4 minutes, stirring as they begin to set, until they are firm but still slightly runny in places.

- Scatter over the feta, then place the pan under the preheated grill for 4–5 minutes or until the omelette is puffed up and golden.

- Cut into wedges and serve with a crisp green salad, if liked.

---

10 Classic Greek Salad
Thinly slice 2 red onions, 4 tomatoes and 1 cucumber and place in a wide salad bowl with 200 g (7 oz) cubed feta cheese and 100 g (3½ oz) pitted black olives. Drizzle over 6 tablespoons of olive oil and sprinkle over 1 teaspoon dried oregano. Season, toss to mix well and serve.

20 Warm Greek-Style Pasta Salad
Cook 250 g (8 oz) short-shaped pasta according to the packet instructions. Meanwhile, roughly chop 2 small red onions, 100 g (3½ oz) pitted black olives, 4 tomatoes and ½ cucumber and place in a salad bowl with a handful of chopped mint leaves. Make a dressing by whisking together 1 crushed garlic clove, 6 tablespoons olive oil, 2 tablespoons vinegar, 1 teaspoon mustard and 1 teaspoon dried oregano, and then season. Drain the pasta and add to the salad with the dressing. Toss to mix well and serve warm.

Beetroot Pasta with Herbs

Serves 4

375 g (12 oz) quick-cook pasta
400 g (13 oz) cooked beetroot
200 ml (7 fl oz) crème fraîche
4 tablespoons chopped chives
4 tablespoons chopped dill
salt and pepper

- Cook the pasta according to the packet instructions.

- Meanwhile, finely dice the beetroot and add to the pasta for the last minute of the cooking time.

- Drain the pasta and beetroot and return to the saucepan. Stir in the crème fraîche and herbs.

- Season and serve immediately.

Speedy Beetroot and Herb 'Risotto'

Blend 250 g (8 oz) roughly chopped cooked beetroot with 6 tablespoons double cream and 100 ml (3½ fl oz) vegetable stock in a food processor until fairly smooth. Stir-fry 1 crushed garlic clove and 1 finely chopped onion in a frying pan with 3 tablespoons olive oil for 3–4 minutes until softened. Add the beetroot mixture and 500 g (1 lb) cooked basmati rice and stir-fry over a high heat for 4–5 minutes or until piping hot. Season with salt and pepper and stir in a small handful each of chopped chives and dill. Serve with a dollop of crème fraîche, diced beetroot and chopped dill.

Spiced Beetroot Pilaf

Heat 2 tablespoons each of oil and butter in a heavy-based saucepan and stir-fry 2 chopped shallots and 1 chopped garlic clove for 1–2 minutes over a medium heat. Add 1 cinnamon stick, 3 teaspoons cumin seeds, 1 teaspoon curry powder, 1 teaspoon crushed coriander seeds, 400 g (13 oz) quick-cook basmati rice, 300 g (10 oz) finely diced cooked beetroot and 1 finely diced carrot and stir to mix well. Add 900 ml (1½ pints) hot vegetable stock, season well and bring up to the boil. Cover tightly and reduce the heat to low. Cook for 10–12 minutes without lifting the lid. Remove from the heat and allow to stand, undisturbed, for 10 minutes. Remove the lid, fluff up the rice grains with a fork and serve.

30 Green Vegetable Curry

Serves 4

1 tablespoon sunflower oil
3 tablespoons Thai green
   curry paste
2 red chillies (optional for hotter
   curry)
1 x 400 ml (14 fl oz) can
   coconut milk
200 ml (7 fl oz) vegetable stock
6 kaffir lime leaves or 1 tablespoon
   finely grated lime zest
2 tablespoons soy sauce
1 tablespoon soft brown sugar
200 g (7 oz) carrots
250 g (8 oz) butternut squash
100 g (3½ oz) sugarsnap peas
10 tablespoons very finely
   chopped coriander leaves
juice of 1 lime
steamed Jasmin rice, to serve

- Deseed and finely slice the chillies, if using. Peel the carrots and cut into thick batons. Peel and deseed the butternut squash, then cut the flesh into 1.5 cm (¾ in) cubes.

- Heat the oil in a large nonstick wok or saucepan. Add the curry paste and chillies, if using, and stir-fry for 2–3 minutes.

- Stir in the coconut milk, stock, lime leaves or lime zest, soy sauce, sugar, carrots and butternut squash. Simmer, uncovered for 6–8 minutes, stirring occasionally.

- Add the sugarsnaps and continue to simmer for 4–5 minutes.

- Remove from the heat and stir in the coriander and lime juice.

- Serve ladled into warmed bowls accompanied by steamed Jasmin rice.

---

10 Mild Thai Green Vegetable Soup

Place 1 tablespoon Thai green curry paste in a saucepan with 400 ml (14 fl oz) coconut milk and 300 ml (10 fl oz) vegetable stock. Bring to the boil and add 200 g (7 oz) sugarsnap peas, 200 g (7 oz) peas and 400 g (13 oz) sweetcorn kernels. Cook for 5–6 minutes, then remove from the heat and stir in 6 tablespoons chopped coriander and squeeze over the juice of 1 lime. Serve immediately.

20 Thai Green Vegetable Rice

Heat 1 tablespoon sunflower oil in a large wok or frying pan and add 2 sliced shallots and 200 g (7 oz) each of finely diced carrots, butternut squash and sliced sugarsnap peas. Stir-fry over a high heat for 4–5 minutes and then add 2 tablespoons Thai green curry paste and 200 ml (7 fl oz) coconut milk. Stir and cook over a high heat for 4–5 minutes and then add 500 g (1 lb) cooked basmati rice. Stir and cook for 3–4 minutes or until well mixed and piping hot. Scatter over a small handful of chopped coriander, season and serve.

30 Rustic Italian-Style Mushrooms with Soft Polenta

Serves 4

150 g (5 oz) polenta

1 tablespoon finely chopped rosemary leaves

1 tablespoon finely chopped sage leaves

8 tablespoons finely chopped flat leaf parsley

8 tablespoons butter

1.5 litres (2½ pints) hot vegetable stock

750 g (1½ lb) large Portobello mushrooms, thickly sliced

3 garlic cloves, crushed

8 tablespoons soft cheese with garlic and herbs

½ teaspoon crushed dried red chilli

salt and pepper

- Place the polenta, rosemary, sage, half the parsley and half the butter in a saucepan over a medium heat and gradually whisk in the stock, stirring continuously.

- Reduce the heat to low, season well and stir constantly until the polenta becomes very thick and starts bubbling (this will take about 6–8 minutes). Remove from the heat and keep warm.

- Meanwhile, heat the remaining butter in a large nonstick frying pan over a high heat. Add the mushrooms and garlic and stir-fry for 6–8 minutes. Season well and stir in the soft cheese and dried chilli. Stir-fry for 2–3 minutes until bubbling. Remove from the heat and stir in the remaining parsley.

- Serve immediately on warmed plates over the polenta.

 Creamy Mushroom and Herb Pasta

Cook 375 g (12 oz) quick-cook pasta according to the packet instructions. Meanwhile heat a large frying pan over a high heat and add 2 tablespoons butter, 2 finely chopped garlic cloves and 750 g (1½ lb) thinly sliced Portobello mushrooms. Stir-fry over a high heat for 3–4 minutes and then stir in 200 g (7 oz) soft cheese with garlic and herbs. Season, toss to mix well and stir in 3 tablespoons chopped parsley. Serve over the pasta.

 Mixed Mushrooms on Grilled Polenta

Cut a 500 g (1 lb) pack of ready-made polenta into thick slices and set aside. Heat 3 tablespoons butter in a large frying pan. Add 750 g (1½ lb) mixed sliced mushrooms and 1 tablespoon thyme leaves. Season well and cook for 6–8 minutes. Increase the heat and add 2 chopped garlic cloves. Cook for 30 seconds, then pour in 50 ml (2 fl oz) red wine and cook for a further 2 minutes. Meanwhile grill the polenta slices under a preheated medium-hot grill for 1–2 minutes on each side. Divide between 4 serving plates. Top with the mushrooms and a dollop of crème fraîche and serve.

30 Herby Quinoa Taboulleh with Olives and Cucumber

Serves 4

1 cucumber, peeled, halved, deseeded and thinly sliced
1 red onion, thinly sliced
juice of 1 lemon
juice of ½ an orange
200 g (7 oz) quinoa
600 ml (1 pint) vegetable stock
1 tablespoon olive oil
4 tablespoons each of chopped coriander, mint and parsley
100 g (3½ oz) green olives, pitted
100 g (3½ oz) mild Peppadew peppers, drained and roughly chopped
salt and pepper

- Place the cucumber and red onion in a bowl, season well and pour over the lemon and orange juices. Cover and set aside.

- Rinse the quinoa thoroughly under cold water in a sieve. Drain and place in a heavy-based saucepan over a medium heat. Cook, stirring continuously, for 3–4 minutes or until the grains separate and begin to brown.

- Add the stock and bring to the boil, stirring continuously. Reduce the heat and cook for 15 minutes, or until the liquid is absorbed. Transfer to a wide serving bowl and drizzle over the olive oil.

- Spoon over the cucumber and red onion mixture with its juices and stir in the chopped herbs, olives and Peppadew peppers.

- Check seasoning, toss to mix well and serve.

---

10 **Herby Rice Salad**
Replace the quinoa in the recipe above with 300 g (10 oz) cooked and cooled microwaveable rice. In addition, stir in 200 g (7 oz) sprouted mixed beans and 12 sliced radishes to the cucumber mixture. Toss to mix well and serve.

20 **Herby Cucumber and Olive Soup with Quinoa** Place 1 litre (1¾ pints) hot vegetable stock in a saucepan with 2 finely diced cucumbers, 100 g (3½ oz) chopped green olives and 100 g (3½ oz) chopped Peppadew peppers. Boil, uncovered, for 12–15 minutes and then stir in 50 g (2 oz) of cooked quinoa. Season and serve immediately.

 # Spinach, Cherry Tomato and Blue Cheese Pasta Salad

Serves 4

400 g (13 oz) cooked and cooled macaroni (or any short-shaped pasta)
50 g (2 oz) baby spinach
400 g (13 oz) halved cherry tomatoes
4 sliced spring onions
200 ml (7 fl oz) ready-made blue cheese dressing
salt and pepper

- Place the cooked and cooled macaroni in a salad bowl with the spinach, cherry tomatoes and spring onions.
- Drizzle over the blue cheese dressing.
- Season to taste, toss to mix well and serve immediately.

 Cheesy Spinach and Tomato Pasta

Cook 375 g (12 oz) macaroni according to the packet instructions. Meanwhile heat a 350 g (11½ oz) tub of ready-made fresh cheese sauce according to the instructions and pour into a large saucepan with 300 g (10 oz) halved cherry tomatoes and 100 g (3½ oz) baby spinach. Stir to mix well and cook over a low heat or until the spinach has wilted. Toss in the drained pasta, season and serve immediately.

 Macaroni Cheese with Spinach and Tomatoes Cook 275 g (9 oz) macaroni in a large saucepan of boiling salted water for 8–10 minutes, drain well and set aside. Meanwhile, melt 40 g (1½ oz) butter over a medium heat in a heavy-based saucepan. Add 40 g (1½ oz) plain flour and stir to form a roux, cooking for a few minutes. Warm 600 ml (1 pint) milk separately. Whisk in the warmed milk, a little at a time. Cook for 10–15 minutes until the sauce is thick and smooth. Stir in 100 g (3½ oz) finely chopped baby spinach leaves and 100 g (3½ oz) cherry tomatoes and season well. Remove from the heat, add 200 g (7 oz) Cheddar cheese and stir until the cheese is well combined and melted. Add the macaroni and mix well. Transfer to a deep ovenproof dish. Sprinkle over 50 g (2 oz) Cheddar cheese and place under a preheated hot grill. Cook until the cheese is browned and bubbling. Serve immediately.

30 Mixed Bean Kedgeree

Serves 4

4 eggs
2 tablespoons olive oil
1 onion, chopped
2 tablespoons mild curry powder
250 g (8 oz) long grain rice
750 ml (1¼ pints) vegetable stock
2 x 400 g (13 oz) cans mixed
   beans, drained and rinsed
150 ml (¼ pint) soured cream

To garnish

2 tomatoes, finely chopped
3 tablespoons chopped
   fresh herbs

- Hard boil the eggs, then plunge into cold water to cool. Shell, cut into wedges and set aside.

- Meanwhile, heat the oil and fry the onion for about 3–4 minutes, until soft.

- Stir in the curry powder and rice, then add the stock. Bring to the boil, cover and simmer for 10–15 minutes until the rice is cooked.

- Stir through the beans and soured cream. Season to taste and serve topped with the eggs and garnish with the tomatoes and herbs.

10 Mixed Bean, Tomato and Rice

Salad Place 2 x 400 g (13 oz) cans mixed beans in a wide bowl with 4 chopped tomatoes, 1 chopped red onion, 4 tablespoons chopped dill and 250 g (8 oz) cooked long grain rice. Mix 1 teaspoon mild curry powder with 200 ml (7 fl oz) ready-made fresh French salad dressing, pour over the salad, toss to mix well and serve.

20 Spiced Bean and Rice Broth

Heat 1 tablespoon olive oil in a saucepan and add 1 chopped onion and 1 tablespoon curry powder and stir-fry for 1–2 minutes. Stir in 1 litre (1¾ pints) hot vegetable stock, 2 x 400 g (13 oz) cans mixed beans, 2 chopped tomatoes and 75 g (3 oz) long grain rice. Bring to the boil and cook, uncovered, for 15 minutes or until the rice is tender. Season, stir in 4 tablespoons chopped coriander and serve ladled into warmed bowls.

30 Kale and Pecorino Pesto Linguini

Serves 4

375 g (12 oz) linguini
300 g (10 oz) kale
2 tablespoons olive oil
3 garlic cloves, crushed
100 g (3½ oz) toasted pine nuts
100 g (3½ oz) mascarpone
  cheese
100 g (3½ oz) pecorino cheese,
  grated, plus extra shavings
  to garnish
½ teaspoon grated nutmeg
salt and pepper

- Cook the pasta according to the packet instructions.

- Meanwhile, wash the kale well, remove any tough stems and chop roughly.

- Heat the oil in a pan and sauté the garlic for 2–3 minutes. Add the kale to the pan. Cover and cook for 2–3 minutes, or until the kale starts to wilt.

- Place the pine nuts into a food processor or blender and whizz until smooth. Tip in the mascarpone, pecorino and nutmeg. Whizz again.

- Add the kale and garlic mixture and whizz until smooth. Season to taste.

- Drain the pasta and return it to the pan. Add the pesto and toss to mix well. Serve garnished with shavings of pecorino.

10 Tomato and Pesto Soup

Heat 2 x 400 g (13 oz) cans cream of tomato soup until piping hot and ladle into shallow soup plates. Swirl 4 tablespoons Kale and Pecorino pesto (from the recipe above) into each serving and scatter over 100 g (3½ oz) ready-made croutons and serve immediately.

20 Kale and Pecorino Pasta Frittata

Mix together 400 g (13 oz) cooked linguini with 4 beaten eggs and 10 tablespoons Kale and Pecorino Pesto (from the recipe above). Season well. Preheat the grill to medium-high. Heat 2 tablespoons olive oil in a large frying pan and add the pasta mixture. Flatten the mixture with a spoon and cook over a medium heat for 8–10 minutes then place under the preheated grill for 4–5 minutes or until golden. Serve immediately with a crisp green salad.

Mixed Bean and Tomato Chilli

Serves 4

2 tablespoons olive oil
1 onion, finely chopped
4 garlic cloves, crushed
1 teaspoon dried red chilli
2 teaspoons ground cumin
1 teaspoon cinnamon
1 x 400 g (13 oz) can chopped
  tomatoes
1 x 400 g (13 oz) can mixed beans,
  rinsed and drained
1 x 400 g (13 oz) can red kidney
  beans in chilli sauce
salt and pepper

To serve

4 tablespoons soured cream
25 g (1 oz) finely chopped
  coriander, to garnish
griddled corn tortillas

- Heat the oil in a heavy-based saucepan and add the onion and garlic. Stir-fry for 3–4 minutes then add the chilli, cumin and cinnamon.

- Stir-fry for 2–3 minutes then stir in the tomatoes. Bring the mixture to the boil, reduce the heat to medium and simmer gently for 10 minutes.

- Stir in the beans and cook for 3–4 minutes until warmed through. Season well and served ladled into 4 warmed bowls.

- Top each serving with a tablespoon of soured cream, garnish with chopped coriander and serve immediately with corn tortillas.

 Mixed Bean, Tomato and Chilli Bruschettas Place ½ onion in a food processor with 2 crushed garlic cloves, 1 teaspoon dried red chilli flakes, 100 g (3½ oz) chopped tomatoes, 1 x 400 g (13 oz) can mixed beans, drained, and 4 tablespoons chopped flat leaf parsley. Whizz until fairly smooth, season and spread the mixture on to toasted ciabatta or sliced sourdough bread, drizzle with a little olive oil and serve.

Mexican Tortilla Grill Place the chilli mixture from the recipe above into a lightly greased, medium-sized ovenproof dish. Layer the top with 200 g (7 oz) tortilla chips. Whisk together 200 ml (7 fl oz) soured cream with 3 eggs and pour over the tortilla chip layer. Sprinkle over 100 g (3½ oz) grated Cheddar cheese and bake in a preheated oven, 220°C (425°F), Gas Mark 7, for 15 minutes or until bubbling and lightly golden. Serve warm or at room temperature.

 # Pasta with Asparagus, Beans and Pesto

Serves 4

400 g (13 oz) short-shaped pasta

200 g (7 oz) asparagus tips, halved

200 g (7 oz) fine green beans, halved

2 tablespoons olive oil

2 tablespoons fresh or ready-made breadcrumbs

6 tablespoons crème fraîche

6 tablespoons ready-made pesto

4 tablespoons Parmesan cheese, grated

salt and pepper

- Bring a large pan of salted water to the boil. Add the pasta and cook according to the packet instructions, adding the asparagus and beans for the last 2 minutes of the cooking time.

- Heat the oil in a small frying pan and fry the breadcrumbs with a pinch of salt until golden.

- Drain the pasta and vegetables, then return to the pan along with the crème fraiche, pesto and a generous grinding of pepper.

- Serve in warmed bowls, scattered with the crispy breadcrumbs and freshly grated Parmesan.

 ### Asparagus, Pesto and Potato Salad

Place 400 g (13 oz) blanched asparagus tips in a bowl with 400 g (13 oz) boiled and halved baby new potatoes and 300 g (10 oz) halved cherry tomatoes. Mix together 200 g (7 oz) crème fraîche with 6 tablespoons ready-made pesto, season and pour over the salad mixture. Toss to mix well and serve.

Asparagus and Green Bean Risotto with Pesto

Heat 2 tablespoons each olive oil and butter in a heavy-based saucepan. When the butter is foaming, add 1 chopped onion and 2 chopped garlic cloves and cook for 2–3 minutes, until beginning to soften. Add 375 g (12 oz) risotto rice, 200 g (7 oz) asparagus tips and 200 g (7 oz) halved green beans. Stir well and cook for a 1–2 minutes then add 150 ml (5 fl oz) dry white wine and simmer for 1 minute, stirring continuously. Reduce the heat and ladle in 1.2 litres (2 pints) hot vegetable stock, 1 ladleful at a time, stirring continuously until each amount is absorbed and the rice is creamy but still firm to the bite. Remove from the heat and stir in 50 g (2 oz) grated Parmesan and 4 tablespoons of fresh pesto. Season well and serve immediately.

30 Ranch-Style Eggs

Serves 4

2 tablespoons olive oil

1 onion, finely sliced

1 red chilli, deseeded and finely chopped

1 garlic clove, crushed

1 teaspoon ground cumin

1 teaspoon dried oregano

400 g (13 oz) canned cherry tomatoes

200 g (7 oz) roasted red and yellow peppers in oil (from a jar), drained and roughly chopped

4 eggs

salt and pepper

4 tablespoons finely chopped coriander, to garnish

- Heat the oil in a large frying pan and add the onion, chilli, garlic, cumin and oregano.

- Fry gently for about 5 minutes or until soft then add the tomatoes and peppers and cook for a further 5 minutes. If the sauce looks dry, add a splash of water.

- Season well and make 4 hollows in the mixture, break an egg into each and cover the pan. Cook for 5 minutes or until the eggs are just set.

- Serve immediately, garnished with chopped coriander.

---

10 Spicy Mexican-Style Scrambled

Eggs Heat 1 tablespoon each olive oil and butter in a large frying pan. Whisk together 8 eggs with 1 crushed garlic clove, 1 finely chopped red chilli, 1 teaspoon dried oregano and 1 teaspoon ground cumin. Season, pour into the frying pan and cook over a medium-low heat, stirring often or until the eggs are scrambled and cooked to your liking. Serve with warm tortillas and garnish with chopped coriander.

20 Mexican-Style Sauce

Heat 2 tablespoons olive oil in a large frying pan and add 1 finely chopped onion, 1 finely chopped red chilli, 1 teaspoon each of ground cumin and dried oregano, 2 x 400 g (13 oz) cans cherry tomatoes and 200 g (7 oz) chopped roasted red peppers in oil (from a jar, drained). Season, bring to the boil and cook over a medium heat for 12–15 minutes. Stir in a small handful of chopped coriander and serve over cooked pasta or rice.

30 Rigatoni with Fresh Tomato, Chilli, Garlic and Basil

Serves 4

6 large ripe plum tomatoes
1 tablespoon extra-virgin olive oil
2 cloves of garlic, finely diced
1 red chilli, deseeded and
  finely diced
75 ml (3 fl oz) vegetable stock
25 g (1 oz) fresh basil leaves,
  finely chopped
375 g (12 oz) dried rigatoni
grated Parmesan cheese,
  to serve (optional)
salt and pepper

- Place the tomatoes in a bowl and pour over boiling water to cover. Leave for 1–2 minutes, then drain, cut across the stem end of each tomato, and peel off the skins.

- When cool enough to handle, cut the tomatoes in half horizontally and shake or gently spoon out the seeds then finely dice the flesh.

- Heat the oil in a large, nonstick frying pan and add the garlic and chilli. Cook on a medium-low heat for 1–2 minutes or until the garlic is fragrant but not browned.

- Add the tomatoes, stock and basil, season well and cook gently for 6–8 minutes or until thickened, stirring often.

- Meanwhile, cook the rigatoni according to the packet instructions, drain and toss into the tomato sauce mixture.

- Spoon into warmed bowls and serve with grated Parmesan, if desired.

 No-Cook Fresh Tomato, Chilli and Basil Sauce Finely chop 6 ripe plum tomatoes and place in a bowl with 2 crushed garlic cloves, 1 finely chopped red chilli and 50 g (2 oz) finely chopped basil leaves. Pour over 8 tablespoons extra virgin olive oil and season well. Serve over cooked pasta, couscous or rice.

 Tomato, Chilli and Mozzarella Pasta Bake Preheat the oven to 220°C (425°F), Gas Mark 7. Place 500 g (1 lb) cooked rigatoni in a shallow ovenproof dish and spoon over 2 x 350 g (11½ oz) tubs of fresh ready-made tomato and basil sauce. Season, add a finely chopped red chilli, toss to mix well and then top with 400 g (13 oz) sliced mozzarella cheese. Bake for 15–20 minutes or until golden and bubbling. Serve immediately.

30 Spinach Dhal with Cherry Tomatoes

Serves 4

300 g (10 oz) red split lentils
200 ml (7 fl oz) coconut milk
600 ml (1 pint) vegetable stock
1 teaspoon ground cumin
1 teaspoon ground coriander
1 teaspoon turmeric
1 teaspoon ground ginger
300 g (10 oz) spinach, chopped
200 g (7 oz) cherry tomatoes
¼ teaspoon garam masala
25 g (1 oz) coriander (leaves and
   stalks), finely chopped
salt and pepper
naan bread or rice, to serve

For the tarka

2 tablespoons sunflower oil
4 shallots, thinly sliced
3 garlic cloves, thinly sliced
1 teaspoon finely chopped ginger
¼ teaspoon chilli powder
2 teaspoons cumin seeds
1 teaspoon black mustard seeds

- Place the lentils in a sieve and rinse under cold running water until the water runs clear. Drain and transfer to a wide saucepan with the coconut milk, stock, cumin, coriander, turmeric and ginger. Bring the mixture to the boil, skimming off any scum as it rises to the surface, and then cover. Reduce the heat and simmer for 15–20 minutes, stirring occasionally to prevent the mixture from sticking to the base of the saucepan.

- Stir in the spinach and cherry tomatoes and cook for 6–8 minutes, or until the lentils are soft and tender, adding a little stock or water if the mixture seems too thick.

- Meanwhile make the tarka. Heat the oil in a small frying pan and sauté the shallots, garlic, ginger, chilli powder, and cumin and mustard seeds, stirring often. Cook for 3–4 minutes until the shallots are lightly browned, and then scrape this mixture into the cooked lentils.

- Stir in the garam masala and chopped coriander, then check the seasoning. Serve with naan bread or rice.

 Lentil, Tomato and Spinach Dhal Soup
Heat 2 x 400 g (13 oz) cans classic lentil soup in a large saucepan with 200 g (7 oz) baby spinach, 1 tablespoon mild curry powder and 200 g (7 oz) halved cherry tomatoes. Bring to the boil and simmer for 2–3 minutes until piping hot. Serve ladled into bowls and topped with a dollop of natural yogurt.

 Spicy Cherry Tomato and Spinach Curry Whizz
2 tablespoons each of grated fresh root ginger and garlic with 200 g (7 oz) plum tomatoes in a blender. Heat 100 ml (3½ fl oz) sunflower oil in a large frying pan, add 400 g (13 oz) cherry tomatoes and stir-fry for 1–2 minutes. Remove with a slotted spoon and drain on kitchen paper. Pour 1 tablespoon oil into the pan and add 2 teaspoons each of fennel and nigella seeds. Stir-fry for 1–2 minutes, then add the ginger, garlic and tomato mixture with 75 g (3 oz) chopped spinach. Stir-fry until the spinach is wilted and then add 1 teaspoon each of ground coriander, turmeric and paprika. Season. Add the cherry tomatoes and cook over a medium heat, stirring, for 6–8 minutes until smooth and thick. Serve with naan bread or chapattis.

30 Romanesco Cauliflower Cheese

Serves 4

8 baby romanescos or 500 g
(1 lb) large cauliflower florets
40 g (1¼ oz) butter, plus extra
for greasing
500 ml (17 fl oz) whole milk
40 g (1¼ oz) plain flour
2 bay leaves
a pinch of freshly grated nutmeg
300 g (10 oz) mature farmhouse
Cheddar, grated
4 tablespoons grated Parmesan
cheese
salt and pepper

· Trim the base of each romanesco to flatten and then lightly butter a shallow, ovenproof dish.

· To make the sauce, melt the butter in a heavy-based saucepan. Gently heat the milk in a separate saucepan. Stir the flour into the melted butter and cook on a low heat for 2–3 minutes, stirring from time to time. Remove the pan from the heat and pour in a little of the warmed milk, stirring continuously. Gradually add the rest of the milk, again stirring continuously. Add the bay leaves and nutmeg and season well. Return the pan to a low heat and cook for 10–12 minutes (or until there is no taste of flour), stirring frequently. Remove the bay leaves. Stir in the Cheddar and remove from the heat.

· Preheat the grill to medium-high.

· Meanwhile, cook the romanescos or cauliflower florets in boiling water for about 5–6 minutes. Drain well, then place in the prepared dish and pour over the sauce.

· Sprinkle over the Parmesan and cook under a preheated grill for 1 minute until lightly browned. Serve immediately.

 Cheat's Cauliflower and Mustard Cheese
Heat 400 g (13 oz) ready-made béchamel sauce according to the instructions with 4 tablespoons grated Cheddar cheese. Meanwhile blanch 875 g (1¾ lb) cauliflower florets for 5–6 minutes or until just tender and place in a serving bowl. Mix 2 tablespoons Dijon mustard with the heated sauce and pour over the cauliflower. Season, toss to mix well and serve with crusty bread.

 Creamy Cauliflower Soup
Place 500 g (1 lb) cauliflower florets, 1 chopped onion and 1 crushed garlic clove in a saucepan with 900 ml (1½ pints) hot vegetable stock. Bring to the boil, cover and cook over a medium heat for 12–15 minutes. Add 300 ml (½ pint) double cream and bring back to the boil. Remove from the heat and whizz using a hand-held blender until smooth. Season and stir in

200 g (7 oz) grated Cheddar cheese just before serving.

Stir-Fried Vegetable Rice

Serves 4

2 tablespoons sunflower oil
6 spring onions, cut diagonally into 2.5 cm (1 in) lengths
2 garlic cloves, crushed
1 teaspoon finely grated fresh root ginger
1 red pepper, deseeded and finely chopped
1 carrot, peeled and finely diced
300 g (10 oz) peas
500 g (1 lb) cooked, white long grain rice
1 tablespoon dark soy sauce
1 tablespoon sweet chilli sauce
chopped coriander and mint leaves, to garnish

- Heat the oil in a large, nonstick wok and add the spring onions, garlic and ginger. Stir-fry for 4–5 minutes and then add the red pepper, carrot and peas. Stir-fry over a high heat for 3–4 minutes.

- Stir in the rice, soy and sweet chilli sauces and stir-fry for 3–4 minutes or until the rice is heated through and piping hot.

- Remove from the heat and serve immediately, garnished with the chopped herbs.

 Veggie Noodle Stir-Fry

Heat 2 tablespoons oil in a wok and add a 300 g (10 oz) pack of prepared stir-fry vegetables. Stir-fry for 2–3 minutes over a high heat and then add 2 x 300 g (10 oz) packs fresh egg noodles and 1 x 125 g (4 oz) sachet ready-made stir-fry sauce. Stir-fry for 1–2 minutes or until piping hot and serve immediately.

 Chinese Vegetables, Szechuan-Style Heat 2 tablespoons vegetable oil in a wok or deep frying pan and add 3 chopped shallots, 2 thinly sliced chillies, 2 teaspoons each of grated fresh root ginger and garlic, 1 teaspoon crushed Szechuan peppercorns and a pinch of salt. Fry for 1 minute, add 150 g (5 oz) diced firm tofu and stir-fry for another 2 minutes, then remove to a plate. Cut 1 carrot into julienne and 2 red peppers into thin strips. Halve 200 g (7 oz) mangetout lengthways. Heat 2 tablespoons sunflower oil and stir-fry the vegetables until starting to wilt, then add 4 tablespoons light soy sauce and 2 tablespoons Shaohsing rice wine. Return the tofu and flavourings to the wok or pan and toss everything together. Drizzle with 1 tablespoon sesame oil and serve with cooked egg noodles or ready-made fried rice.

 # Tomato and Aubergine Pappardelle

Serves 4

4 tablespoons extra virgin olive oil

1 large aubergine, cut into 1.5 cm (¾ in) dice

1 small onion, finely diced

2 garlic cloves, crushed

1 x 350 g (11½ oz) jar tomato and basil pasta sauce

375 g (12 oz) dried pappardelle or tagliatelle

250 g (8 oz) buffala mozzarella cheese, drained and diced

To garnish

4 tablespoons grated Parmesan cheese (optional)

basil leaves, to garnish (optional)

- Put a large pan of salted water on to boil.

- Heat the oil in a large frying pan over a medium-high heat. Add the aubergine and onion and cook, stirring, for 5 minutes.

- Add the garlic and cook for 1 minute. Add the tomato sauce and 200 ml (7 fl oz) water to the pan, bring to a simmer and cook for 8–10 minutes, or until the aubergines are just tender. Season to taste.

- Meanwhile, cook the pasta according to the packet instructions. Remove from the heat, drain, and return to the pan.

- Stir the mozzarella into the sauce until it begins to melt and become stringy, then add to the pasta. Toss to mix well, sprinkle over the Parmesan and garnish with basil leaves, if desired.

 1 **Tomato, Aubergine and Mozzarella Pizzas** Preheat the oven to 220 °C (425 °F), Gas Mark 7. Place 2 ready-made pizza bases on 2 baking sheets and spread over the tomato and aubergine sauce from the above recipe. Scatter over 250 g (8 oz) diced mozzarella and place in the oven for 8–10 minutes. Serve immediately.

 2 **Grilled Aubergine, Tomato and Basil Salad** Thinly slice 2 large aubergines and brush with olive oil. Cook in a preheated griddle pan over a high heat for 2–3 minutes on each side or until tender. Transfer to a platter with 4 large, ripe, sliced tomatoes and 250 g (8 oz) sliced buffala mozzarella cheese. Whisk together 6 tablespoons olive oil with 1 crushed garlic clove and the juice of 1 lemon. Season and drizzle over the salad. Scatter over a handful of basil leaves and serve.

# Tex-Mex Sweetcorn Salad

Serves 4

400 g (13 oz) sweetcorn kernels

400 g (13 oz) roasted red peppers (from a jar), drained and sliced

1 finely chopped red onion

4 tablespoons chopped jalapeno peppers (from a jar)

1 x 400 g (13 oz) can red kidney beans, drained

4 tablespoons chopped parsley

6 tablespoons ready-made salad dressing

salt and pepper

- Place the sweetcorn kernels in a bowl with the peppers, onion, jalapeno peppers and kidney beans. Scatter over the chopped parsley.

- Drizzle over the salad dressing, season, toss to mix well and serve immediately.

 Sweetcorn, Red Pepper and Potato Hash Bring a pan of salted water to the boil and cook 400 g (13 oz) diced potatoes for 5 minutes. Drain well. Heat 2 tablespoons each oil and butter in a large, deep frying pan over a medium heat. Add the potatoes and cook for 5–6 minutes, turning once. Add 1 diced red pepper and fry for 2–3 minutes. Add 400 g (13 oz) sweetcorn to the pan and stir in 1 chopped red chilli, 6 sliced spring onions and 2 sliced garlic cloves. Season and cook for 5 minutes until cooked through. Meanwhile, fry 4 eggs until cooked to your liking and serve the hash on warmed plates topped with the eggs.

Sweetcorn and Red Pepper Frittata Heat 2 tablespoons olive oil in a medium, nonstick frying pan and place over a medium heat. Add 1 finely chopped red onion and stir-fry for 2–3 minutes. Stir in 200 g (7 oz) frozen peas and cook for 1–2 minutes. Add 1 x 400 g (13 oz) can sweetcorn kernels (drained), and 1 x 400 g (13 oz) jar roasted red peppers (drained and roughly chopped) and stir-fry for 1–2 minutes. Preheat the grill to medium. Pour 4 lightly beaten eggs over the mixture, season well and sprinkle over 4 tablespoons finely chopped parsley. Cook over a gentle heat for 10 minutes or until the base of the frittata is set. Remove from the heat and place the pan under the grill for 3–4 minutes or until the top is set and lightly golden. Cut into thick wedges and serve warm or at room temperature, with a salad.

30 Smoked Cheese, Pepper and Spinach Quesadillas

Serves 4

300 g (10 oz) baby spinach

200 g (7 oz) roasted red peppers (from a jar), drained and roughly chopped

8 spring onions, trimmed and finely chopped

200 g (7 oz) smoked cheese, finely diced

150 g (5 oz) mild Cheddar cheese, grated

1 red chilli, deseeded and finely chopped

4 tablespoons finely chopped coriander leaves

8 soft corn tortillas

salt and pepper

olive oil, for greasing

soured cream, to serve

- Blanch the spinach in a large saucepan of lightly salted boiling water for 1–2 minutes. Drain thoroughly through a fine sieve, pressing out all the liquid. Transfer to a bowl with the roasted pepper, spring onions, smoked cheese, Cheddar, chilli and coriander. Season and mix well.

- Scatter a quarter of the spinach mixture over a tortilla, top with another tortilla and press together. Make 3 more quesadillas in the same way.

- Grease 2 large frying pans with a little olive oil and place over a medium heat. Put 1 quesadilla into each pan and cook for 2 minutes until golden. Invert on to a plate, then slide back into the pan and cook for another 2 minutes, until the filling is hot and the cheese is just melting. Set aside while you cook the other 2.

- Cut each quesadilla into 4 and serve with soured cream.

 Pepper, Spinach and Egg Noodle Stir-Fry Heat 3 tablespoons light olive oil in a large wok or frying pan and add 8 sliced spring onions, 2 crushed garlic cloves, 1 sliced red chilli and 400 g (13 oz) drained and sliced roasted red peppers (from a jar) and 300 g (10 oz) baby spinach and stir-fry for 4–5 minutes over a high heat or until the spinach has just wilted. Stir in 400 g (13 oz) cooked fresh egg noodles and 6 tablespoons sweet chilli sauce, and cook for 1–2 minutes or until piping hot.

 Spicy Spinach, Pepper and Smoked Cheese Burgers Heat 2 tablespoons olive oil in a large wok or frying pan and add 6 finely sliced spring onions and 200 g (7 oz) baby spinach. Stir-fry for 5–6 minutes or until the spinach has wilted. Season and set aside. Split 4 burger buns, lightly toast and spread 2 tablespoons of mayonnaise on each half. Divide 200 g (7 oz) drained and sliced roasted peppers (from a jar) between the 4 burger bases and top each with the spinach mixture and 2 slices of smoked cheese. Cover with the 4 toasted bun tops, press down lightly and serve.

Herby Bulgar and Chickpea Salad

Serves 4

400 g (13 oz) can chickpeas, drained

100 g (3½ oz) cooked bulgar wheat

200 g (7 oz) roasted red peppers (from a jar), drained and chopped

large handful chopped dill

large handful chopped coriander

6 tablespoons olive oil

juice of 1 orange

1 teaspoon ground cumin

salt and pepper

- Place the chickpeas in a bowl with the bulgar wheat and peppers. Add the dill and coriander.

- Whisk together the olive oil, orange juice and cumin and season well. Pour the dressing over the salad, toss to mix well and serve immediately.

 Herbed Middle Eastern Chickpea Pilaf Heat 2 tablespoons each butter and oil in a heavy-based saucepan and add 1 chopped red onion, 2 chopped garlic cloves, 2 teaspoons ground cumin, 1 teaspoon ground cinnamon and cook for 1–2 minutes. Add 400 g (13 oz) easy-cook basmati rice, a 400 g (13 oz) can chickpeas, drained, 4 tablespoons finely chopped dill and 900 ml (1½ pints) hot vegetable stock. Season well, bring to the boil, cover and reduce the heat to low. Cook for 10 minutes and then leave to stand for 8–10 minutes. Fluff up the grains with a fork and serve.

Turkish Chickpea and Bulgar Pilaf Heat 2 tablespoons olive oil in a large saucepan. Add 1 finely chopped red onion and fry over a medium-low heat for 10–12 minutes, stirring often, or until the onion is lightly golden. Stir in 1 crushed garlic clove, 1 teaspoon ground cumin, 1 teaspoon ground cinnamon and 175 g (6 oz) bulgar wheat and cook, stirring, for 1–2 minutes to lightly toast the grains. Pour over 350 ml (12 fl oz) hot vegetable stock, stir well, then bring to the boil. Cover and reduce the heat to medium-low and gently simmer for 6–8 minutes or until all the liquid is absorbed. Remove from the heat and add 200 g (7 oz) roasted red peppers from a jar (drained and roughly chopped) and a 400 g (13 oz) can chickpeas (without stirring them in). Cover and allow to stand for 5–10 minutes. Just before serving, remove the lid from the pilaf and fluff up the grains with a fork, mixing in the red pepper and chickpeas. Carefully fold in 25 g (1 oz) each finely chopped dill and flat leaf parsley, along with 2 tablespoons finely chopped mint leaves. Finally scatter over goats' cheese. Season to taste and serve hot, warm or cold.

Cold Asian Summer Soba Noodle Salad

Serves 4

625 g (1¼ lb) cooked soba
  noodles
2 carrots, finely julienned
6 spring onions, finely shredded
1 red pepper, finely sliced
4 tablespoons dark soy sauce
3 tablespoons sesame oil
1 tablespoon mirin
1 tablespoon caster sugar
½ teaspoon chilli oil

- Place the soba noodles in a wide bowl with the carrots, spring onions and pepper.

- In a separate bowl, mix together the soy sauce, sesame oil, mirin, sugar and chilli oil, then pour over the noodle mixture.

- Toss to mix well and serve chilled or at room temperature.

 Warm Noodle and Soy Bean Salad

Bring a large saucepan of lightly salted water to the boil and add 250 g (8 oz) soba noodles and 250 g (8 oz) frozen podded soya beans and cook according to the packet instructions for the noodles. Drain and return to the saucepan with 6 sliced spring onions. Cover and keep warm. Mix together 1 teaspoon grated fresh root ginger, 1 red chilli, deseeded and finely chopped, 1 tablespoon toasted sesame oil, 3 tablespoons mirin, 3 tablespoons light soy sauce and 1 teaspoon clear honey. Pour over the noodle mixture and mix well. Sprinkle over 2 tablespoons toasted sesame seeds and 4 tablespoons finely chopped coriander and serve.

 Soba Noodle and Shiitake Mushroom Soup Cook 250 g (8 oz) soba noodles according to the packet instructions. Divide the noodles between 4 serving bowls. Meanwhile, place 1 litre (1¾ pints) hot vegetable stock, 3 tablespoons mirin, 200 g sliced shiitake mushrooms and 5 tablespoons dark soy sauce in a saucepan and bring to the boil. Add 200 g (7 oz) halved sugarsnap peas and continue to cook for 4–5 minutes, or until the sugarsnaps are cooked. Taste for seasoning, adding more soy sauce if liked. Ladle the broth with some mushrooms and sugarsnaps over the soba noodles in the bowls and sprinkle with sliced spring onions to serve.

Tortellini, Roasted Pepper and Rocket Salad

Serves 4

2 x 250 g (8 oz) ready-made fresh spinach and ricotta tortellini

400 g (13 oz) roasted red and yellow peppers in oil (from a jar), drained

100 g (3½ oz) rocket leaves

1 red onion, thinly sliced

200 ml (7 fl oz) fresh Italian-style salad dressing

black pepper

- Cook the tortellini according to the packet instructions.

- Meanwhile chop the peppers and place in a bowl with the rocket leaves and onion. Add the cooked tortellini.

- Pour over the salad dressing, toss to mix well and serve sprinkled with black pepper.

2 Tortellini and Red Pepper Grill

Preheat the grill to medium-high. Place 2 x 250 g (8 oz) cooked ready-made fresh spinach and ricotta tortellini in a lightly greased shallow ovenproof dish. Stir in 400 g (13 oz) chopped roasted red and yellow peppers in oil (from a jar), drained, and 400 g (13 oz) can chopped tomatoes with garlic and herbs, and toss to mix well. Season and pour over a 350 g (11½ oz) tub ready-made fresh cheese sauce to cover. Place under the grill for 4–5 minutes or until the top is golden and bubbling. Serve warm with a rocket salad.

3 Red and Yellow Pepper Tortellini

Cut 1 red and 1 yellow pepper into large pieces, removing the seeds and membrane. Place skin side up under a hot grill until the skin blackens and blisters. Cool in a plastic bag, then peel away the skin. Roughly chop the white sections of 8 spring onions and place in a food processor with the peppers and 2 chopped cloves garlic and pulse until chopped. Cook 2 x 250 g (8 oz) ready-made fresh spinach and ricotta tortellini in a large saucepan of boiling water according to the packet instructions. Drain and return to the pan. Toss the pepper mixture into the pasta, add 6 tablespoons olive oil and 40 g (1½ oz) Parmesan cheese. Season to taste. Garnish with extra spring onions and serve.

30 Creamy Mushroom and Herb Pancakes

Serves 4

2 tablespoons butter, plus extra
for greasing

300 g (10 oz) baby chestnut
mushrooms, sliced

6 spring onions, finely sliced

2 garlic cloves, crushed

500 g (1 lb) tub fresh four-
cheese sauce

300 g (10 oz) baby spinach leaves

4 tablespoons finely chopped
parsley

2 tablespoons finely chopped
tarragon

8 ready-made savoury pancakes

50 g (2 oz) Parmesan, grated

salt and pepper

lettuce leaves, to serve

- Heat the butter in a large, nonstick frying pan, add the mushrooms, spring onions and garlic and stir-fry over a high heat for 6–7 minutes.

- Stir in half of the cheese sauce and heat until just bubbling. Add the spinach and cook for 1 minute until just wilted. Set aside, stir in the chopped herbs and season.

- Take 1 pancake and spoon one-eighth of the filling down the centre. Carefully roll the pancake up and put into a shallow, buttered gratin dish. Repeat with the remaining pancakes. Drizzle the remaining cheese sauce over the pancakes, sprinkle with grated Parmesan and season to taste. Cook under a preheated medium-high grill for 3–4 minutes, until piping hot and turning golden.

- Remove from the heat and serve with lettuce leaves.

 Creamy Mushroom Spaghetti

Cook 375 g (12 oz) quick-cook spaghetti according to the packet instructions. Meanwhile whizz 300 g (10 oz) chestnut mushrooms in a blender with 500 g (1 lb) tub ready-made fresh four-cheese sauce, then tip into a large saucepan and bring to the boil. Simmer for 2–3 minutes and then stir in 4 tablespoons chopped tarragon. Drain the pasta and add to the mushroom mixture, mix well, season and serve straight away.

 Cheesy, Garlic and Herb Stuffed Mushrooms Trim and remove the stalks from 8 large flat mushrooms and finely chop the stalks. Heat 2 tablespoons butter in a nonstick frying pan and add the chopped mushroom stalks, 4 chopped spring onions and 1 crushed garlic clove. Stir-fry over a high heat for 6–8 minutes. Season well and transfer to a bowl with 200 g (7 oz) cottage cheese, 1 tablespoon lemon zest and 3 tablespoons each of chopped parsley and tarragon. Place the mushroom caps gill side up on a grill rack in a single layer and season well. Divide the stuffing among the caps and then sprinkle over 50 g (2 oz) grated Parmesan. Position the grill rack about 12 cm (5 in) under a preheated medium-high grill and cook for 6–8 minutes or until the tops are golden and bubbling. Line 4 serving plates with 50 g (2 oz) spinach leaves, top each plate with 2 stuffed mushrooms and serve immediately.

Special
Occasions

Recipes listed by cooking time

3

2

30 Jewelled Fruity Spicy Pilaf

Serves 4

1 tablespoon saffron threads
1 litre (1¾ pints) hot vegetable stock
400 g (13 oz) basmati rice
1 tablespoon olive oil
1 tablespoon butter
3 shallots, finely chopped
2 cloves garlic, finely chopped
4 cardamom pods, lightly bruised
2 cloves
2 cinnamon sticks
2 teaspoons cumin seeds
2 carrots, peeled and finely diced
4 tablespoons chopped dill
300 g (10 oz) podded soya beans
100 g (3½ oz) golden sultanas
100 g (3½ oz) dried cranberries
seeds from 1 ripe pomegranate
50 g (2 oz) slivered pistachio nuts
salt and pepper

- Add the saffron to the hot stock and set aside.

- Rinse the rice in cold running water and leave to drain.

- Heat the oil and butter in a heavy-based saucepan and stir-fry the shallots and garlic for 1–2 minutes over a medium heat.

- Add the cardamom pods, cloves, cinnamon sticks, cumin seeds, rice and carrots and stir to mix well. Add the stock mixture along with the dill, season and bring up to the boil. Then stir in the soya beans, golden sultanas and dried cranberries. Cover tightly and reduce the heat to low. Cook for 10–12 minutes without lifting the lid.

- Remove from the heat and allow to stand, undisturbed, for 10 minutes.

- Remove the lid (the liquid should have been completely absorbed), stir in the pomegranate seeds and pistachio nuts and serve immediately.

 Fruity Spiced Couscous

Place 400 g (13 oz) cooked couscous in a wide bowl with 1 finely julienned carrot, 2 finely sliced shallots, 100 g (3½ oz) golden sultanas, 100 g (3½ oz) chopped dill and 100 g (3½ oz) pomegranate seeds. Whisk together 6 tablespoons olive oil with the juice of 1 orange, 1 teaspoon each of ground cinnamon and cumin and pour over the couscous mixture. Season, toss to mix well and serve.

 Stir-Fry Fruity, Nutty Rice

Heat 2 tablespoons each butter and vegetable oil in a large wok or frying pan. Add 1 thinly sliced onion and cook over a medium-low heat for 10–12 minutes or until lightly golden. Stir in 500 g (1 lb) cooked long-grain or basmati rice with 100 ml (3½ fl oz) vegetable stock and stir-fry over a high heat for 4–5 minutes. Stir in 100 g (3½ oz) golden sultanas, 100 g (3½ oz) dried cranberries, 100 g (3½ oz) pistachio nuts and 100 g (3½ oz) toasted pine nuts. Stir-fry for 1–2 minutes or until piping hot and well mixed. Season and serve with natural yogurt.

30 Asparagus and Fontina Cheese Crespelles

Serves 4

750 g (1½ lb) asparagus, woody
  ends trimmed
3 tablespoons olive oil
15 g (½ oz) Parmesan, freshly
  grated, plus extra to sprinkle
500 g (1 lb) tub ready-made
  white sauce
freshly grated nutmeg, to taste
12 ready-made savoury pancakes
125 g (4 oz) Fontina cheese, plus
  extra for sprinkling

- Place the asparagus in a roasting tin, toss with the oil and roast in a preheated oven, 240°C (475°F), Gas Mark 9, for 7 minutes or until tender. Set aside.

- Reduce the oven temperature to 220°C (425°F), Gas Mark 7.

- Stir the Parmesan into the white sauce and season with nutmeg. Spread a little sauce on to a pancake, top with asparagus and Fontina. Roll up and place into a 2-litre (3½-pint) ovenproof dish. Repeat with the remaining pancakes.

- Drizzle the remaining sauce over the pancakes in the dish, sprinkle with the extra cheese and nutmeg. Bake for 12–15 minutes or until golden. Serve immediately.

---

10 Grilled Asparagus Bruschettas with Melted Fontina

Blanch 625 g (1¼ lb) asparagus tips in a saucepan of lightly salted boiling water for 2–3 minutes. Drain and divide the asparagus between 8 slices of toasted sourdough bread and scatter over 200 g (7 oz) grated Fontina cheese. Grill under a preheated medium grill for 2–3 minutes or until the cheese has just melted. Season and serve with a crisp green salad.

20 Herbed Asparagus and Fontina Souffléd Custards

Lightly grease the insides of 4 ramekins with melted butter. Heat 2 tablespoons butter in a frying pan and stir-fry 200 g (7 oz) chopped asparagus and 6 chopped spring onions for 3–4 minutes, then drain thoroughly in a metal sieve to remove the excess moisture and pat dry. Meanwhile, put 4 egg whites into a bowl and whisk until just stiff. In a separate bowl, beat 4 egg yolks and add the asparagus mixture, 6 tablespoons each of chopped dill and chives and 200 g (7 oz) grated Fontina cheese. Stir in 1 tablespoon Dijon mustard, season and, using a metal spoon, fold in the egg whites. Spoon the mixture into the ramekins, almost to the top. Bake in a preheated oven, 220°C (425°F), Gas Mark 7, for 12–15 minutes or until risen and lightly set. Serve immediately with a crisp lettuce and tomato salad.

Broccoli and Mushrooms in Black Bean Sauce with Noodles

Serves 4

1 tablespoon sunflower oil
1.5 cm (¾ in) piece of fresh root ginger, sliced into matchsticks
200 g (7 oz) small broccoli florets
200 g (7 oz) shiitake mushrooms
6 spring onions, sliced into 1.5 cm (¾ in) lengths
1 red pepper, deseeded and sliced
300 ml (½ pint) vegetable stock
500 g (1 lb) fresh egg noodles
2 tablespoons light soy sauce
1 tablespoon cornflour mixed to a paste with 2 tablespoons water

For the black bean sauce

1 tablespoon fermented salted black beans, rinsed well
1 tablespoon light soy sauce
2 garlic cloves, crushed
1 red chilli, deseeded and chopped
1 tablespoon Shaohsing rice wine

- Place all the ingredients for the black bean sauce in a food processor, blend until fairly smooth and set aside.

- Heat a wok over high heat and add the oil. When smoking, add the ginger and stir-fry for a few seconds. Add the broccoli and stir-fry for a further 2–3 minutes.

- Add the mushrooms, spring onions and red pepper and stir-fry for 2–3 minutes.

- Tip in the black bean sauce and vegetable stock and bring to a simmer. Cook for 2–3 minutes until tender.

- Meanwhile, cook the noodles according to the packet instructions, drain and keep warm.

- Season with soy sauce to taste, mix in the blended cornflour paste and cook to thicken for 1 minute. Serve immediately with the egg noodles.

 Broccoli, Mushroom and Black Bean Stir-Fry Heat 1 tablespoon vegetable oil in a large wok and add 300 g (10 oz) broccoli florets, 300 g (10 oz) sliced shiitake mushroom and 6 sliced spring onions. Stir-fry over a high heat for 3–4 minutes and then add a 125 g (4 oz) sachet of ready-made black bean stir-fry sauce and 100 ml (3½ fl oz) water. Stir-fry over a high heat for 3–4 minutes and serve over noodles.

 Oriental Mushroom, Broccoli and Black Bean Rice Heat 2 tablespoons oil in a heavy-based saucepan and add 2 teaspoons each grated fresh root ginger and garlic, 8 sliced spring onions, 300 g (10 oz) sliced shiitake mushrooms and 300 g (10 oz) broccoli florets. Stir-fry for 3–4 minutes and then add 300 g (10 oz) long-grain rice. Stir to mix well and pour over 750 ml (1¼ pints) hot vegetable stock and 200 g (7 oz) can black beans, drained. Season, bring to a boil, cover tightly and reduce the heat to low. Cook for 10–12 minutes, then remove from the heat (keeping the lid on) and allow to stand for a further 10 minutes. Stir in 4 tablespoons light soy sauce, fluff up the grains of rice and serve immediately.

3⬤ Tagliatelle with Pumpkin and Sage

Serves 4

875 g (1¾ lb) pumpkin, butternut
   or winter squash, peeled,
   deseeded and cut into 1.5 cm
   (¾ in) cubes
4 tablespoons olive oil
500 g (1 lb) fresh tagliatelle
50 g (2 oz) rocket leaves
8 sage leaves, chopped
grated Parmesan cheese, to serve
   (optional)
salt and pepper

· Place the pumpkin into a small roasting tin, add
  2 tablespoons of the olive oil, season and toss to mix
  well. Roast in a preheated oven, 220 °C (425 °F), Gas
  Mark 7, for 15–20 minutes or until just tender.

· Meanwhile, bring a large pan of salted water to the boil.
  Cook the pasta according to the packet instructions.
  Drain, return to the pan, then add the rocket, sage and
  pumpkin. Mix together over a gentle heat with the remaining
  olive oil until the rocket has wilted, then serve with a good
  grating of fresh Parmesan cheese, if desired.

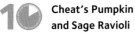

1⬤ Cheat's Pumpkin and Sage Ravioli

Cook 2 x 250 g (8 oz) packs fresh
pumpkin-filled ravioli according
to the packet instructions.
Meanwhile heat 4 tablespoons
butter and 4 tablespoons olive
oil in a large frying pan with
2 chopped garlic cloves and
6 sage leaves over a medium low
heat. Drain the ravioli and add to
the pan. Season and toss gently
to mix well and serve, sprinkled
with 100 g (3½ oz) grated
Parmesan cheese.

2⬤ Roasted Pumpkin, Tomato and Sage

Soup Place the roasted pumpkin
from the above recipe into a
saucepan with 600 ml (1 pint)
hot vegetable stock, 200 ml
(7 fl oz) passata and 1 tablespoon
finely chopped sage leaves.
Bring to the boil and simmer for
12–15 minutes. Using a hand-held
blender, whizz the mixture until
smooth. Stir in 100 ml (3½ fl oz)
double cream and serve with
warmed crusty bread.

30 Vegetable Pad Thai

Serves 4

300 g (10½ oz) flat rice noodles
3 tablespoons tamarind paste
3 tablespoons light soy sauce
3 tablespoons palm sugar
4 tablespoons vegetable oil
500 g (1 lb) firm tofu, cut into
    5 mm (¼ in) strips, patted dry
3 garlic cloves, finely chopped
2 shallots, finely chopped
300 g (10½ oz) Oriental
    mushrooms, torn or sliced
1–2 red chillies, deseeded and
    finely chopped
2 large eggs, beaten
bunch of spring onions, sliced
1 carrot, halved and finely sliced
handful of fresh chives, snipped
bunch of fresh coriander, chopped
100 g (3½ oz) chilli roasted peanuts
2 limes, cut into wedges

- Place the noodles in a large bowl and cover with warm water. Leave to soak for 10–15 minutes or until soft, then drain.

- Meanwhile, make the sweet-and-sour paste. Mix the tamarind paste with a little hot water to loosen. Add the soy sauce and palm sugar; mix, taste and adjust to give a nice combination of sweet, salty and sour.

- Heat 2 tablespoons of the oil in a wok or large frying pan. Fry the tofu for 3–4 minutes until golden and beginning to crisp. Remove from the wok, keep warm and set aside.

- Heat the remaining oil in the wok and fry the garlic and shallots for 30 seconds. Add the mushrooms and red chilli and cook for 2 minutes until beginning to soften. Add the noodles and stir-fry for 2 minutes, then push to one side.

- Add the eggs and allow them to set, then scramble and mix with the noodles. Tip in the sweet-and-sour paste and stir well. Toss in the onions, carrot and tofu and cook for a few minutes.

- Divide among warmed serving bowls, sprinkle with the herbs and peanuts, and serve with the lime wedges.

---

10 Thai Vegetable Salad Julienne 1 carrot, 8 spring onions and 1 cucumber and place in a large bowl with 2 thinly sliced Thai shallots and 300 g (10½ oz) diced firm tofu. Make a dressing from the juice of 2 limes, 4 tablespoons fish sauce, 3 tablespoons light soy sauce, 4 tablespoons sweet chilli sauce and 1 crushed garlic clove. Pour the dressing over the salad, season and toss well. Garnish with 100 g (3½ oz) chopped roasted peanuts and serve.

20 Vietnamese-Style Vegetable Noodle Salad Place 5 chopped garlic cloves in a bowl with 50g (2 oz) chopped coriander leaves and 1 finely chopped red chilli. Add the juice of 1 lime, 4 tablespoons light soy sauce, 3 tablespoons fish sauce and 3 tablespoons caster sugar. Stir to mix and allow the sauce to sit for 5 minutes. Bring a large pan of salted water to the boil. Add 375 g (12 oz) thin rice noodles and cook for 2 minutes. Drain well and rinse the noodles with cold water to cool. Drain again. Combine the sauce mixture and noodles with 2 julienned carrots, 1 shredded cucumber and 4 tablespoons chopped mint in a large serving bowl. Toss well and serve the salad garnished with 100 g (3½ oz) chopped roasted peanuts.

 **Tarragon and Cheddar Cheese Soufflé Omelette**

Serves 4

6 eggs
4 tablespoons chopped tarragon
100 g (3½ oz) strong Cheddar
  cheese, grated
2 tablespoons unsalted butter
crisp salad and crusty bread, to
  serve

- Separate the eggs and set aside the yolks. In a clean bowl, whisk the egg whites until stiff.

- Place the egg yolks in a separate bowl with the tarragon and Cheddar cheese and lightly beat.

- Heat the butter in a large heavy-based frying pan. Carefully fold the egg white mixture into the egg yolk mixture and add to the pan. Cook for 2–3 minutes over a high heat and then place under a preheated medium-hot grill for 3–4 minutes or until the top is souffléd and lightly golden.

- Serve immediately with a crisp salad and crusty bread.

 Cheesy, Tarragon and Pasta Gratin

Place 400 g (13 oz) cooked fusilli pasta in a lightly greased, shallow ovenproof dish. Whisk together 4 eggs, 4 tablespoons finely chopped tarragon, ¼ teaspoon cayenne pepper, 2 teaspoons Dijon mustard and 200 g (7 oz) grated Cheddar cheese. Pour over the pasta, toss to mix well. Sprinkle over 100 g (3½ oz) grated Parmesan and bake in a preheated oven, 220°C (425°F), Gas Mark 7, for 15 minutes or until lightly golden on top. Serve immediately.

Cheese and Tarragon Soufflés

Brush 4 x 300 ml (½ pint) ramekins with melted butter and sprinkle with 100 g (3½ oz) Parmesan. Melt 50 g (2 oz) butter in a pan and add 40 g (1½ oz) plain flour, ½ teaspoon English mustard powder and good pinch of cayenne pepper. Cook for a couple of minutes, then gradually add 300 ml (½ pint) milk, stirring continuously, until the mixture comes to the boil. Boil for 2 minutes until very thick. Remove from the heat, stir in 100 g (3½ oz) strong

Cheddar cheese, grated, 4 tablespoons tarragon, chopped, and 4 egg yolks and season well. In a clean bowl, whisk 4 egg whites until stiff. Using a metal spoon, carefully fold the egg whites into the cheese mixture. Spoon into the ramekins, just up to the rim. Run your finger around the inside edge of the ramekins to help the soufflés rise straight up. Put on a preheated baking sheet in a preheated oven, 220°C (425°F), Gas Mark 7, and bake for 10–12 minutes or until risen and golden. Serve immediately with a crisp salad.

Ravioli with Sweet Potato, Tomatoes and Rocket

Serves 4

50 g (2 oz) butter

375 g (12 oz) peeled sweet potato, cut into 1 cm (½ in) cubes

2 garlic cloves, chopped

small handful of fresh sage leaves, chopped

grated zest of ½ lemon, plus a squeeze of juice

200 g (7 oz) cherry tomatoes, halved

2 x 250 g (8 oz) packs ready-made fresh cheese-filled ravioli

salt and pepper

To serve

100 g (3½ oz) soft goats' cheese, crumbled

large handful rocket leaves

- Melt half the butter in a large frying pan, add the chopped sweet potato, season well, then fry over a medium heat for about 5–6 minutes until golden brown all over.

- Add the garlic, sage and lemon zest and fry for 1 minute.

- Add the remaining butter, the cherry tomatoes and the lemon juice and gently fry over a low heat for 1 minute until melted.

- Meanwhile, cook the ravioli according to the packet instructions. Drizzle with a little olive oil, then add the cooked pasta to the pan with the sweet potato and cherry tomatoes, and carefully stir to coat with the sauce.

- Spoon into serving bowls and scatter with the goats' cheese, rocket leaves and black pepper before serving.

 Rocket, Tomato and Ravioli Pasta Salad Cook 2 x 250 g (8 oz) packs ready-made fresh cheese-filled ravioli according to the packet instructions, drain under cold water and then place in a wide salad bowl with a large handful of rocket, 100 g (3½ oz) crumbled goats' cheese and 200 g (7 oz) halved cherry tomatoes. Whisk together 6 tablespoons olive oil with 1 crushed garlic clove and the juice of 1 lemon. Season, pour over the salad and toss to mix well before serving.

Lemony Sweet Potato, Ravioli and Cherry Tomato Bake Cook 2 x 250 g (8 oz) packs fresh ready-made cheese-filled ravioli according to the packet instructions, drain and add to a medium-sized, lightly greased baking dish along with 300 g (10 oz) halved cherry tomatoes and 200 g (7 oz) finely diced sweet potato. In a bowl, whisk together 3 eggs with 300 ml (½ pint) double cream, 2 tablespoons lemon zest, 1 crushed garlic clove, 2 teaspoons finely chopped sage leaves and 100 g (3½ oz) crumbled soft goats' cheese. Pour over the ravioli mixture and bake in a preheated oven, 200°C (400°F), Gas Mark 6, for 20 minutes or until golden and bubbling. Serve immediately with a rocket salad.

Deep-Fried Haloumi Beer-Batter Fritters

Serves 4

250 g (8 oz) plain flour
1 egg, separated
300 ml (½ pint) ice-cold lager
125 ml (4 fl oz) ice-cold water
vegetable oil, for deep-frying
500 g (1 lb) haloumi

To serve

rocket leaves
lemon wedges

- Sift the flour into a large bowl and add the egg yolk. Gradually whisk in the lager, then add the measured water and whisk until well combined.

- Whisk the egg white in a separate bowl until stiff peaks form. Fold this into the batter.

- Fill a deep-fat fryer or a large, deep, heavy-based saucepan two-thirds full with vegetable oil. Heat the oil to 180 °C (350°F) or until a cube of bread turns golden in 10–15 seconds.

- Cut the haloumi into 1 cm (½ in) slices, then dip in the batter to coat. Fry the haloumi in batches for 3–4 minutes, or until crisp and golden-brown. Remove with a slotted spoon, season and serve on rocket leaves with wedges of lemon to squeeze over.

Mixed Pepper and Haloumi Skewers

Cut 2 red peppers, 2 yellow peppers, 2 red onions and 300 g (10 oz) haloumi cheese into bite-sized pieces. Place the vegetables and cheese in a wide bowl. Mix together 2 crushed garlic cloves, 8 tablespoons olive oil, 2 teaspoons dried thyme and the juice and finely grated zest of 1 lemon. Pour over the cheese and vegetables and toss to mix. Thread the vegetables and cheese alternately on to 12 metal skewers. Season and grill under a preheated medium–high grill for 4–5 minutes on each side. Serve immediately.

Grilled Haloumi with Roasted Peppers

Cut 250 g (8 oz) haloumi cheese into slices 2.5 cm (1 in) long and 5 mm (¼ in) thick. Combine 1½ teaspoons ground sumac, 3 teaspoons finely grated lemon zest and 3 tablespoons olive oil in a large bowl. Toss the haloumi gently in the oil mixture to coat, and then season. Heat a griddle pan to medium-high. Slice 2 aubergines lengthways and brush with olive oil. Cook the slices in batches for 2–3 minutes on each side or until lightly charred. Transfer to a wide bowl or platter. Cook the haloumi in the griddle pan for 2–3 minutes on each side or until golden. Toss 200 g (7 oz) roasted red and yellow peppers in oil (from a jar), drained and roughly chopped, with the aubergine gently to combine. Divide among 4 serving plates and top with the haloumi. Whisk the juice of 1 large lemon with 3 tablespoons olive oil in a bowl then season. Drizzle over the salad and serve garnished with 2 tablespoons each of chopped parsley and mint leaves.

30 Malaysian Coconut and Vegetable Stew

Serves 4

2 tablespoons vegetable oil
1 medium onion, thinly sliced
6 tablespoons laksa curry paste
2 x 400 ml (14 fl oz) cans
  coconut milk
300 ml (½ pint) water
1 teaspoon salt
200 g (7 oz) peeled potatoes,
  cut into 1.5 cm (¾ in) pieces
250 g (8 oz) peeled carrots,
  cut into 1.5 cm (¾ in) pieces
100 g (3½ oz) fine green beans,
  topped, tailed and halved
150 g (5 oz) cauliflower florets
300 g (10 oz) peeled and
  deseeded butternut squash, cut
  into 1.5 cm (¾ in) pieces
50 g (2 oz) cashew nuts
50 g (2 oz) beansprouts
4 spring onions, trimmed and
  sliced on the diagonal
handful of Thai sweet basil leaves
  or fresh coriander

- Heat the oil in a large pan over a medium heat. Add the onion and the curry paste and fry gently for 2–3 minutes until it begins to smell fragrant.

- Add the coconut milk, measured water and salt and bring to the boil.

- Add the potatoes and carrots and cook for 10 minutes, then add the green beans, cauliflower and squash and cook for a further 7 minutes.

- Add the cashew nuts and simmer for 3 minutes until the vegetables are just tender.

- Stir in the beansprouts, spring onions and basil or coriander. Simmer for 1 minute and serve immediately.

 Quick Asian Coconut Soup

Heat 1 tablespoon vegetable oil in a large wok and add 6 chopped spring onions, 1 tablespoon laksa curry paste, 400 ml (14 fl oz) can coconut milk, 400 ml (14 fl oz) vegetable stock and 300 g (10 oz) pack stir-fry vegetables. Bring to the boil and cook over a high heat for 4–5 minutes. Season and serve.

 Spicy Coconut and Vegetable Noodles

Heat 1 tablespoon vegetable oil in a large wok or frying pan and add 6 sliced spring onions, 2 garlic cloves, 200 g (7 oz) each finely shredded carrots, mangetout and red pepper. Stir-fry for 4–5 minutes. Meanwhile, soak 375 g (12 oz) dried stir-fry rice noodles according to the packet instructions and then drain. Add 1 tablespoon laksa curry paste to the frying pan and stir-fry for 3–4 minutes and then add 200 ml (7 fl oz) coconut cream along with the drained noodles. Stir-fry for 2–3 minutes, season and serve.

30 Nasi Goreng

Serves 4

2 large eggs

3 tablespoons sunflower oil

1 tablespoon tomato purée

1 tablespoon ketjap manis (sweet dark soy sauce)

625 g (1¼ lb) cooked rice

1 tablespoon light soy sauce

5 cm (2 in) piece cucumber, quartered lengthways and sliced

salt and pepper

8 spring onions, trimmed and thinly sliced on the diagonal, to garnish

For the spice paste

2 tablespoons vegetable oil

4 garlic cloves, roughly chopped

50 g (2 oz) shallots, roughly chopped

25 g (1 oz) roasted salted peanuts

6 medium-hot red chillies, deseeded and roughly chopped

1 teaspoon salt

- To make the spice paste, place all of the ingredients into a small food processor and whizz into a smooth paste, or grind using a pestle and mortar. Beat the eggs and season.

- Heat a little sunflower oil in a small frying pan over a medium-high heat, pour in one-third of the beaten egg and cook until set on top. Flip, cook for a few more seconds then turn out and roll up tightly. Repeat twice more with the remaining egg. Slice the omelettes across into thin strips.

- Heat a wok over a high heat until smoking. Add 2 tablespoons of the oil and the spice paste and stir-fry for 1–2 minutes.

- Add the tomato purée and ketchup manis and cook for a few seconds, then tip in the cooked rice and stir-fry over a high heat for 2 minutes until heated through.

- Add the strips of omelette and stir-fry for another minute before adding the soy sauce, cucumber and most of the spring onions and tossing together well.

- Spoon the nasi goring on to a large warmed plate, scatter over the remaining spring onions and serve.

10 Quick Spicy Rice Broth

Tip 400 g (13 oz) cooked rice into a saucepan with 200 ml (7 fl oz) coconut milk, 600 ml (1 pint) hot vegetable stock, 2 tablespoons tomato purée and 1 tablespoon mild curry powder. Bring to the boil and cook over a high heat for 4–5 minutes. Remove from the heat and stir in 6 finely shredded spring onions and ¼ cucumber, finely shredded. Season and serve in warmed bowls.

20 Indonesian Savoury Egg and Rice 'Cake'

Heat 2 tablespoons oil in a large, nonstick frying pan. Beat 6 eggs in a large bowl with 3 tablespoons tomato purée, 1 tablespoon curry paste, 6 finely sliced spring onions, 1 tablespoon ketjap manis, 6 tablespoons finely chopped coriander and 1 finely chopped red chilli. Add 400 g (13 oz) cooked rice and stir to mix well. Meanwhile, pour the mixture into the frying pan and cook over a medium heat for 8–10 minutes or until the base is lightly golden and set. Transfer to a preheated medium-high grill for 3–4 minutes or until the top is set and golden. Serve immediately.

30 Pesto and Antipasti Puff Tart

Serves 4

375 g (12 oz) pack ready-rolled
  puff pastry
3 tablespoons ready-made pesto
300 g (10 oz) yellow and red
  cherry tomatoes, halved
150 g (5 oz) mixed antipasti
  (artichokes, roasted peppers,
  mushrooms and aubergine),
  from a jar, drained
100 g (3½ oz) goats' cheese,
  crumbled
basil leaves, to serve

- Lay the puff pastry on a baking tray. Score a 2.5 cm (1 in) margin around the edge and prick the base with a fork.

- Top with the pesto, cherry tomatoes, mixed antipasti and goats' cheese. Bake in a preheated oven, 200°C (400°F), Gas Mark 6, for 15–20 minutes.

- Top with the basil leaves and serve.

 Spaghetti with Pesto and Cherry Tomatoes Cook 375 g (12 oz) quick-cook spaghetti according to the packet instructions. Meanwhile, halve 500 g (1 lb) mixed cherry tomatoes and place in a wide bowl with a handful of basil leaves. When the pasta is cooked, drain and add to the tomatoes with 8 tablespoons fresh pesto and garnish with 50 g (2 oz) toasted pine nuts. Toss to mix well, season and serve.

 Antipasti and Pesto Pasta Salad Cook 300 g (10 oz) rigatoni or penne according to the packet instructions. Meanwhile, make the pesto by placing 50 g (2 oz) basil leaves, 25 g (1 oz) toasted pine nuts, 50 g (2 oz) grated Parmesan cheese, 1 crushed garlic clove and 100 ml (3½ fl oz) olive oil in a blender and whizz until fairly smooth. Season with black pepper and place in a wide serving dish with 300 g (10 oz) halved cherry tomatoes, 200 g (7 oz) mixed antipasti (from a jar) and then tip in the cooked pasta. Toss to mix well and serve at room temperature.

30 Flash-in-the-Pan Ratatouille

Serves 4

100 ml (3½ fl oz) olive oil

2 onions, chopped

1 aubergine, cut into 1.5 cm (¾ in) cubes

2 large courgettes, cut into 1.5 cm (¾ in) cubes

1 red pepper, deseeded and cut into 1.5 cm (¾ in) pieces

1 yellow pepper, deseeded and cut into 1.5 cm (¾ in) pieces

2 cloves garlic, crushed

1 x 400 g (13 oz) can chopped tomatoes

2–3 tablespoons balsamic vinegar

1 teaspoon soft brown sugar

10–12 black olives, pitted

salt and pepper

torn basil leaves, to garnish

- Heat the oil in a large pan until very hot and stir-fry all of the vegetables, except the tomatoes, for a few minutes.

- Add the tomatoes, balsamic vinegar and sugar, season and stir well. Cover tightly and simmer for 15 minutes until the vegetables are cooked.

- Remove from the heat, scatter over the olives and torn basil leaves and serve.

 Mediterranean-Style Thick Vegetable Soup Blend the cooked ratatouille from the above recipe with 300 ml (½ pint) hot vegetable stock until fairly smooth. Ladle into warmed bowls and serve garnished with basil leaves.

 Grilled Vegetables Mediterranean-style Thinly slice 2 aubergines and 2 large courgettes lengthways. Brush with olive oil and cook, in batches, on a smoking-hot griddle pan for 2–3 minutes on each side. Transfer to a serving platter and add 300 g (10 oz) drained and sliced roasted red peppers (from a jar), drained, 2 finely chopped tomatoes and 100 g (3½ oz) pitted black olives. In a small bowl, whisk together 8 tablespoons olive oil, 3 tablespoons balsamic vinegar, 1 teaspoon finely chopped rosemary leaves, 1 crushed garlic clove and 1 teaspoon soft brown sugar. Season and pour over the vegetables. Toss to mix well and serve garnished with basil leaves.

30 Roasted Vegetable Couscous Salad

Serves 4

1 red and 1 yellow pepper, deseeded and cut into 2.5 cm (1 in) pieces

1 medium aubergine, cut into 2.5 cm (1 in) pieces

1 courgette, cut into 2.5 cm (1 in) cubes

2 small red onions, peeled and cut into thick wedges

olive oil, to drizzle

200 g (7 oz) couscous

6–8 preserved lemons, halved

a large handful of chopped mint and coriander leaves

50 g (2 oz) pine nuts, toasted

150 g (5 oz) feta cheese, crumbled

100 g (3½ oz) pomegranate seeds

salt and pepper

For the dressing

juice of 1 orange

5 tablespoons olive oil

1 teaspoon ground cumin

½ teaspoon ground cinnamon

salt and pepper

- Place the vegetables on a large nonstick baking tray. Drizzle with a little olive oil and season well. Roast in a preheated oven, 200°C (400°F), Gas Mark 6, for 15–20 minutes, or until the edges of the vegetables are just starting to char.

- Meanwhile, put the couscous in a wide bowl and pour over boiling hot water to just cover. Season well. Cover with clingfilm and allow to stand, undisturbed, for 10 minutes or until all the liquid has been absorbed. Fluff up the grains with a fork and place on a wide, shallow serving platter.

- Make the dressing by mixing together the orange juice, olive oil, cumin and cinnamon and season well.

- Fold the roasted vegetables, preserved lemons and herbs into the couscous, pour over the dressing and toss to mix well.

- Just before serving, scatter over the pine nuts, feta and pomegranate seeds and serve immediately.

Lemon and Herb Couscous

Tip 500 g (1 lb) cooked couscous into a large bowl with 8 tablespoons each chopped mint and coriander, 6 sliced spring onions and 6 chopped preserved lemons. Season, toss to mix well and serve, garnished with toasted pine nuts.

Roasted Vegetable Tabolleh

Roast the vegetables as per the recipe above. While the vegetables are roasting place 200 g (7 oz) fine bulgar wheat in a large bowl and pour over hot vegetable stock until just covered. Cover and allow to stand, undisturbed, for 15 minutes or until tender. Add 2 finely chopped garlic cloves, 6 tablespoons olive oil, a large handful each of chopped flat leaf parsley and mint and the roasted vegetables and their juices. Season, toss to mix well and serve.

20 Spicy Szechuan Tofu and Vegetable Stir-Fry

Serves 4

4 tablespoons vegetable oil
6 spring onions, finely sliced
2 red chillies, thinly sliced
2.5 cm (1 in) piece of fresh
  ginger, finely chopped
4 garlic cloves, finely sliced
1 teaspoon crushed Szechuan
  peppercorns
pinch of salt
250 g (8 oz) firm tofu, cut into
  2.5 cm (1 in) cubes
200 g (7 oz) mangetout, halved
150 g (5 oz) baby sweetcorn,
  halved lengthways
250 g (8 oz) pak choi, chopped
300 g (10 oz) beansprouts
2 tablespoons light soy sauce
2 tablespoons Shaohsing rice wine
sesame oil, for drizzling
cooked rice, to serve

- Heat 2 tablespoons of the oil in a wok or deep frying pan and add the spring onions, chillies, ginger, garlic, peppercorns and a pinch of salt. Fry for 1 minute, add the tofu and stir-fry for another 2 minutes, then transfer to a plate.

- Heat the remaining oil and stir-fry the mangetout, sweetcorn, pak choi and beansprouts for a few minutes, until starting to wilt, then add the soy sauce and rice wine.

- Return the tofu mixture to the wok or pan and toss everything together.

- Drizzle with sesame oil and serve with cooked rice.

10 Szechuan-Style Tofu Stir-Fry

Cube 500 g (1 lb) firm tofu and grill under a preheated medium grill for 2–3 minutes until golden brown. Meanwhile, heat 2 tablespoons vegetable oil in a wok or deep frying pan. Add 2 x 300 g (10 oz) packs stir-fry vegetables and stir-fry for 3–4 minutes. Stir in a 150 g (5 oz) sachet ready-made Szechuan stir-fry sauce and stir-fry for a further 1–2 minutes. Add the tofu to the pan, toss to mix and serve.

30 Noodle and Tofu Salad with Szechuan Peppercorns

In a large bowl mix together 4 tablespoons light soy sauce, 3 tablespoons sweet chilli sauce, finely grated zest and juice of 1 lemon, 2 chopped red chillies, 2 teaspoons Szechuan peppercorns and 2 tablespoons water. Add 500 g (1 lb) firm tofu cubes and leave to marinate for at least 25 minutes. Meanwhile, place 200 g (7 oz) fine rice noodles in a large bowl, cover with boiling water and set aside for 5 minutes. Drain and cool under running water. Toss together the cooled noodles, 100 g (3½ oz) thinly sliced mangetout, 100 g (3½ oz) thinly sliced radishes, 1 thinly sliced red onion and 1 tablespoon toasted sesame seeds. Gently stir in the tofu and marinade and divide between bowls. Scatter over the coriander leaves and serve.

30 Autumnal Moroccan Vegetable Tagine

Serves 4

2 tablespoons olive oil

1 onion, halved and thickly sliced

3 garlic cloves, finely chopped

1 teaspoon finely grated fresh
  root ginger

1 teaspoon cinnamon

pinch of saffron threads

2 teaspoons ground cumin

4 teaspoons harissa paste

4 tablespoons tomato purée

3 tablespoons clear honey

875 g (1¾ lb) mixed autumn
  vegetables, such as squash,
  parsnips and sweet potato,
  peeled and cubed

750 ml (1¼ pints) vegetable stock

salt and pepper

couscous, to serve

chopped coriander, to garnish

- Heat the oil in a large nonstick saucepan and sauté the onion and garlic for 1–2 minutes.

- Add the ginger, cinnamon, saffron, ground cumin, harissa paste, tomato purée, honey, vegetables and stock and bring to the boil.

- Season, cover and simmer for 20 minutes or until the vegetables are very tender.

- Serve with couscous and garnish with the chopped coriander.

 Moroccan-style Couscous Place 400 g (13 oz) couscous in a bowl with 2 teaspoons harissa paste, 1 teaspoon each of ground cumin and cinnamon, a large pinch of saffron, ½ chopped onion, 3 tablespoons tomato purée, 200 g (7 oz) chopped tomatoes and 1 tablespoon clear honey. Pour over hot vegetable stock to just cover. Season, stir, cover and allow to stand for 8 minutes or until all the liquid is absorbed. Fluff up with a fork, stir in 4 tablespoons chopped coriander and serve.

 Moroccan-style Root Vegetable Pasta Sauce Heat 2 tablespoons olive oil in a saucepan and add 1 chopped onion, 2 crushed garlic cloves, 1 teaspoon grated fresh root ginger, 1 teaspoon each of ground cumin and cinnamon and stir-fry for 1–2 minutes. Add 400 g (13 oz) can chopped tomatoes, 2 teaspoons harissa paste and 200 ml (7 fl oz) hot vegetable stock. Stir in 625 g (1¼ lb) finely diced mixed seasonal vegetables (such as squash, sweet potato and swede) and bring to the boil. Cook, uncovered, for 15 minutes or until the vegetables are tender. Season and serve over pasta.

 # Aubergine and Harissa Sauté

Serves 4

4 tablespoons sunflower oil

750 g (1½ lb) baby aubergines, thinly sliced

4 tomatoes, chopped

1 teaspoon ground cinnamon

1 teaspoon finely chopped coriander leaves

2 tablespoons harissa

salt and pepper

cooked basmati rice, to serve

- Heat the oil in a large frying pan and add the aubergines.

- Fry over a high heat for 2–3 minutes then add the tomatoes, cinnamon, coriander and harissa. Stir-fry for 3–4 minutes or until the aubergines are tender.

- Season to taste and serve with basmati rice.

 Crispy Moroccan-Style Aubergine and Harissa Fritters Cut 750 g (1½ lb) aubergines into thin batons and mix in a bowl with 2 tablespoons harissa paste, 1 teaspoon turmeric, 1 teaspoon crushed coriander and some salt. Add 250 g (8 oz) chickpea flour, a little at a time, stirring to coat the aubergine. Gradually drizzle cold water over the mixture, adding just enough to make a sticky batter. Fill a deep saucepan one-quarter full with sunflower oil and place over a high heat until it reaches 180°C (350°F) or a cube of bread it sizzles and turns golden in 10–15 seconds. Fry spoonfuls of the mixture in batches for 1–2 minutes or until golden brown and crisp on the outside. Remove with a slotted spoon and drain on kitchen paper. Serve with a minted yogurt dip.

 Braised Baby Aubergines with Honey and Harissa Place 1 tablespoon finely grated fresh root ginger, 2 tablespoons finely grated garlic and half a 400 g (13 oz) can chopped tomatoes in a blender and whizz until smooth. Heat 100 ml (3½ fl oz) sunflower oil in a large, heavy-based frying pan and cook 625 g (1¼ lb) halved baby aubergines in batches over a medium heat, in a single layer, for 6–8 minutes or until lightly browned, turning once. Remove with a slotted spoon and drain on kitchen paper. Reheat the oil left in the frying pan and add 1 teaspoon ground cumin, 2 teaspoons fennel seeds and 2 teaspoons nigella seeds. Stir-fry for 1–2 minutes and then add the blended ginger, garlic and tomato mixture. Stir-fry for 2–3 minutes and then add the remaining tomatoes from the can along with 1 teaspoon ground cinnamon, 1 teaspoon ground coriander and 1 tablespoon rose harissa. Season well. Cook over a medium heat, stirring often, for 10 minutes or until the mixture is smooth and thick. Stir in 1 tablespoon clear honey. Transfer the aubergines back to the pan, toss gently to coat evenly, cover and cook gently for 3–4 minutes. Remove from the heat and scatter over 2 tablespoons toasted pine nuts and 6 tablespoons chopped coriander. Serve with couscous or rice.

 # Broccoli and Blue Cheese Soufflés

Serves 4

50 g (2 oz) butter, plus extra
  melted butter for greasing
handful of fine fresh white
  breadcrumbs
250 g (8 oz) broccoli florets
40 g (1½ oz) plain flour
300 ml (½ pint) milk
1 teaspoon smoked paprika
grated fresh nutmeg
4 large eggs, separated
100 g (3½ oz) creamy blue
  cheese, crumbled
salt and pepper

- Brush 4 x 300 ml (½ pint) ramekins with melted butter and sprinkle with breadcrumbs to coat the base and sides.

- Blanch the broccoli in boiling water until almost tender, then pulse in a blender until smooth.

- Melt the butter in a pan, add the flour and cook for 2 minutes. Gradually add the milk, stirring continuously, and bring to the boil. Boil for 2 minutes, until very thick.

- Remove from the heat and stir in the spices and egg yolks. Season well and stir in the puréed broccoli and cheese.

- In a clean bowl, whisk the egg whites until stiff. Using a metal spooon, carefully fold the egg whites into the broccoli and cheese mixture.

- Pour into the ramekins, almost up to the rim. Run your finger around the inside edge of the ramekins to help the soufflés rise straight up. Bake on a preheated hot baking sheet in a preheated oven, 200°C (400°F), Gas Mark 6, for 8–10 minutes or until risen. Serve immediately.

 Thick Broccoli and Blue Cheese Soup Place 1 x 600 g (1 lb 3 oz) tub ready-made fresh vegetable soup in a saucepan with 400 g (13 oz) finely chopped broccoli florets and bring to the boil. Simmer, uncovered, for 5–6 minutes and then blend with a hand-held blender until fairly smooth. Stir in 200 ml (7 fl oz) double cream and 100 g (3½ oz) crumbled creamy blue cheese. Season and serve in warmed bowls with crusty bread.

 Pasta with Griddled Broccoli and Blue Cheese Cook 375 g (12 oz) penne according to the packet instructions. Meanwhile, blanch 500 g (1 lb) broccoli florets in a saucepan of boiling hot water for 3–4 minutes. Drain thoroughly and toss with 4 tablespoons olive oil and grill in a smoking hot griddle pan for 3–4 minutes or until just tender. Drain the pasta and return to the saucepan with the broccoli, 100 g (3½ oz) crumbled creamy blue cheese and 200 g (7 oz) cream cheese. Season well. Sprinkle over 50g (2 oz) chopped toasted walnuts and serve with a rocket salad.

Spring Onion, Dill and Chive Pancakes

Serves 4

175 g (6 oz) plain flour
1 teaspoon baking powder
150 ml (5 fl oz) milk
2 large eggs
50 g (2 oz) butter, melted
2 tablespoons each finely
  chopped dill and chives,
  plus extra to garnish
4 spring onions, finely chopped
vegetable oil, for shallow-frying
salt and pepper

To serve

200 g (7 oz) cream cheese,
  whisked with juice of 1 lemon
2 plum tomatoes, finely chopped

- Sift the flour and baking powder into a bowl with a pinch of salt. Whisk the milk, eggs, butter, herbs and spring onions together in a separate bowl.

- Stir the wet mixture into the dry ingredients until the mixture comes together as a smooth, thick batter.

- Heat a little vegetable oil in a small nonstick frying pan and spoon in one-eighth of the batter. Cook the pancake for 1–2 minutes, or until bubbles form on the surface, then carefully turn it over and cook for a further 1–2 minutes, or until golden-brown on both sides. Remove the pancake and keep warm while the remaining pancakes are cooked; the mixture makes 8 pancakes.

- Stack 2 pancakes on each serving plate and spoon over a dollop of the cream cheese mixture. Top with the chopped tomatoes and serve garnished with a sprinkling of herbs and freshly ground black pepper.

Scrambled Eggs with Dill, Chives and Cream Cheese Whisk together 6 eggs with 200 g (7 oz) cream cheese then add a small handful each of chopped chives and dill. Heat 2 tablespoons butter in a large frying pan and add the egg mixture. Cook, stirring, until the eggs are scrambled. Season and serve over hot buttered toast.

 Middle Eastern Spring Onion and Herb Soup Slice the white and green parts of 750 g (1½ lb) spring onions into 2.5 cm (1 in) lengths and keep separate. Melt 50 g (2 oz) butter in a large saucepan, add 50 ml (2 fl oz) olive oil, white spring onion slices, the 6 halved garlic cloves and then season. Sauté on a medium heat for 4–5 minutes until the vegetables are soft. Toss in the green spring onion segments along with 3 bay leaves and cook for 10 minutes. Add 300 g (10 oz) peas and 1 diced courgette, and cook for a further 5 minutes. Remove half the vegetables from the pan and set aside. Add 1 litre (1¾ pints) stock to the remaining vegetables, bring to the boil and simmer for 3 minutes. Remove the bay leaves and throw in a small handful each of chopped dill and chives. Whizz until smooth with a hand-held blender before returning the reserved vegetables to the pan and warming gently. Stir in 200 g (7 oz) cream cheese until combined. Transfer the soup into individual bowls and serve.

30 Griddled Asparagus with Caper Dressing and Ducks' Eggs

Serves 4

1 tablespoon olive oil, plus extra for drizzling
625 g (1¼ lb) asparagus spears
4 ducks' eggs
4 slices sourdough bread, toasted
2 tablespoons olive oil
200 g (7 oz) medium vine tomatoes
salt and pepper

For the dressing

2 tablespoons capers, rinsed and drained
6 tablespoons olive oil
2 tablespoons red wine vinegar
1 teaspoon Dijon mustard
1 garlic clove, crushed
2 teaspoons crushed pink peppercorns

- Blanch the asparagus spears for 1–2 minutes.

- Place the tomatoes on a baking sheet lined with nonstick baking parchment, drizzle with a little olive oil, season and roast in a preheated oven, 200°C (400°F), Gas Mark 6, for 10–12 minutes.

- Meanwhile, toss the asparagus with the olive oil and heat a griddle pan until smoking. Cook the asparagus for 4 minutes, turning once. Remove and share between 4 serving plates.

- Fry the eggs in a frying pan or until cooked to your liking. Add a slice of toasted sourdough to each plate and top with the fried egg.

- Mix together all the ingredients for the dressing, season and drizzle over the asparagus and eggs.

- Serve immediately with the roasted tomatoes.

 Asparagus, Lettuce and Duck Egg Salad Blanch 625 g (1¼ lb) asparagus tips in a pan of lightly salted boiling water for 3 minutes. Drain and place on a wide platter with 300 g (10 oz) halved or quartered medium vine tomatoes, 2 shelled and quartered, hard-boiled ducks' eggs, and the leaves from 2 little gem lettuces. Make the dressing: whisk together 6 tablespoons olive oil, 2 tablespoons red wine vinegar, 1 teaspoon Dijon mustard and 1 crushed garlic clove and season well. Pour over the salad and toss to mix before serving.

 Spanish-style Asparagus and Vine Tomato Tortilla Cut 625 g (1¼ lb) asparagus tips in half. Using a fork, gently beat 6 eggs in a bowl with 100 g (3½ oz) grated Parmesan cheese and 2 tablespoons chopped basil, then season well. Heat 4 tablespoons olive oil in an ovenproof frying pan over a high heat and add 2 chopped garlic cloves, 6 chopped medium vine tomatoes and the asparagus. Toss together and cook for 2 minutes or until the garlic starts to change colour.

Add the egg mixture to the pan, distributing it evenly without stirring. Once the eggs start to set around the sides, place under a preheated medium-high grill for 3–4 minutes, or until set and golden and fluffy. Serve with a mixed salad.

30 Lemon and Herb Risotto

Serves 4

1 tablespoon olive oil

3 shallots, finely chopped

2 cloves garlic, finely chopped

½ head celery, finely chopped

1 courgette, finely diced

1 carrot, peeled and finely diced

300 g (10 oz) arborio rice

1.2 litres (2 pints) hot vegetable stock

good handful fresh mixed herbs (tarragon, parsley, chives, dill)

100 g (3½ oz) butter

1 tablespoon finely grated lemon zest

100 g (3½ oz) freshly grated Parmesan cheese

salt and pepper

- Heat the oil in a heavy-based saucepan and add the shallots, garlic, celery, courgette and carrot and fry slowly for 4 minutes or until the vegetables have softened. Add the rice and turn up the heat. Stir-fry for 2–3 minutes.

- Add a ladleful of hot stock followed by half the herbs and season well.

- Reduce the heat to medium-low and add the remaining stock, 1 ladleful at at time, stirring constantly until each amount is absorbed and the rice is just firm to the bite but cooked through.

- Remove from the heat and gently stir in the remaining herbs, butter, lemon zest and Parmesan. Place the lid on the pan and allow to sit for 2 to 3 minutes, during which time it will become creamy and oozy. Serve immediately, sprinkled with freshly ground black pepper.

 Lemon and Vegetable Rice

Heat 1 tablespoon olive oil in a large frying pan and add 2 chopped shallots, 2 chopped garlic cloves and a 300 g (10 oz) pack stir-fry vegetables. Add 2 x 250 g (8 oz) packs microwaveable rice and the zest and juice of 1 small lemon. Stir-fry for 5–6 minutes or until piping hot. Serve immediately.

 Lemon and Herb Tagliatelle

Heat 1 tablespoon oil in a large frying pan and add 2 chopped shallots, 1 chopped garlic clove, ½ finely diced carrot and 1 finely diced celery stalk. Sauté over a medium heat for 4–5 minutes. Meanwhile cook 375 g (12 oz) tagliatelle according to the packet instructions. Drain and add to the frying pan with a large handful of chopped mixed herbs along with the juice and finely grated zest of 1 small lemon. Sprinkle over 100 g (3½ oz) grated Parmesan and serve.

Asparagus and Udon Noodle Stir-Fry

Serves 4

2 tablespoons sunflower oil
2 garlic cloves, crushed
400 g (13 oz) asparagus tips
8 spring onions, sliced diagonally
400 g (13 oz) straight-to-wok
   udon noodles
5 tablespoons oyster sauce
5 tablespoons water

- Heat the oil in a large frying pan. Add the garlic and asparagus tips and stir-fry for 2 minutes.

- Add the spring onions, noodles, oyster sauce and water and toss together. Stir-fry for a further 2 minutes, then serve immediately.

 Asparagus, Beans and Udon Noodle Bowl Combine 3 tablespoons dark soy sauce, 2 tablespoons rice vinegar, 1 tablespoon mirin and 2 tablespoons caster sugar in a shallow bowl and stir until the sugar has dissolved. Add 300 g (10 oz) firm tofu, cut into bite-sized cubes and turn to coat. Leave to absorb the flavours for about 15 minutes or more. When ready to cook, turn the oven on to low and heat an ovenproof plate. Scatter 2 tablespoons cornflour over a separate plate. Remove the tofu from the marinade, reserving the marinade, and roll the tofu in the cornflour to coat. Heat a wide frying pan over a medium-high heat and add enough sunflower oil to cover the base. Fry the tofu, using tongs to turn, until dark golden and crisp all over. Drain on kitchen paper, then keep warm by placing on the plate in the oven. Meanwhile, pour 1 litre (1¾ pints) vegetable stock into a medium saucepan with the reserved marinade and bring to the boil. Add 400 g (13 oz) asparagus tips, 50 g (2 oz) soya beans, 50 g (2 oz) frozen peas, 1 teaspoon grated fresh root ginger and 400 g (13 oz) straight-to-the-wok udon noodles and simmer about 3–4 minutes until the vegetables are just tender. Divide between 4 bowls and share out the tofu cubes between each. Top with 25 g (1 oz) roughly chopped coriander leaves and serve drizzled with a little chilli oil.

Udon Noodle Pancakes with Griddled Asparagus Cook 200 g (7 oz) udon noodles according to the packet instructions. Drain and set aside. Heat 2 tablespoons vegetable oil in a frying pan over a high heat. Divide the noodles into 12 portions and fry in batches. Flatten with a spatula, so the surface browns, reduce the heat to medium-high and cook the noodle 'pancakes' for 3–4 minutes or until golden and crispy on the base. Turn and cook for 1–2 minutes more, again flattening as they cook. Remove and keep warm. Heat a griddle pan until smoking. Brush 400 g (13 oz) asparagus tips with oil and sear for 2–3 minutes on each side. Transfer to a bowl and mix with 6 tablespoons oyster sauce and 3 tablespoons sweet chilli sauce. Serve the noodle 'pancakes' immediately topped with the asparagus mixture.

30 Tomato, Camembert, Goats' Cheese and Herb Tart

Serves 4

250 g (8 oz) puff pastry

3–4 tablespoons black olive tapenade or Dijon mustard, if preferred

300 g (10 oz) ripe plum tomatoes, finely sliced

8 large basil leaves, roughly torn

125 g (4 oz) Camembert cheese

100 g (3½ oz) goats' cheese

2 tablespoons fresh thyme leaves, plus extra to garnish

1–2 tablespoons extra virgin olive oil

salt and pepper

- Roll out the pastry and use it to line a 25 cm (10 in) tart tin.

- Spread the tapenade or mustard over the base of the tart.

- Discarding any juice or seeds that have run from the tomatoes, lay the slices in concentric circles in the tart. Season the tomatoes (bear in mind that tapenade is salty) and scatter over the basil.

- Cut the Camembert into thin wedges and the goats' cheese into thin wedges or slices, according to its shape. Arrange a circle of Camembert pieces around the outside and a circle of goats' cheese within. Put any remaining pieces of cheese in the middle.

- Sprinkle over the thyme leaves and drizzle the oil on top.

- Bake in a preheated oven, 200°C (400°F), Gas Mark 6, for 15–18 minutes until the pastry is cooked and the cheese is golden and bubbling. Serve immediately, garnished with thyme.

10 Tomato, Tapenade and Two Cheese Baguette Split 2 warmed baguettes and spread both sides with 10 tablespoons black olive tapenade, 6 tablespoons Dijon mustard and fill each with 400 g (13 oz) ripe, sliced plum tomatoes, 25 g (1 oz) basil leaves, 100 g (3½ oz) each of sliced Camembert cheese and goats' cheese. Season and serve with a green salad.

20 Fresh Tomato and Two Cheese Pasta Cook 375 g (12 oz) farfalle pasta according to the packet instructions. Meanwhile, finely chop 4 plum tomatoes, 100 g (3½ oz) pitted black olives, 25 g (1 oz) basil leaves and 2 tablespoons thyme leaves and place in a bowl with 100 g (3½ oz) each of diced goats' cheese and Camembert cheese. Drain the pasta and add to the tomato mixture. Season, toss to mix well and serve immediately.

30 Butter Bean and Vegetable Nut Crumble

Serves 4

75 g (3 oz) butter, chilled and diced

175 g (6 oz) plain flour

100 g (3½ oz) walnuts, chopped

50 g (2 oz) Cheddar cheese, grated

2 x 250 g (8 oz) packs prepared broccoli, cauliflower and carrots

500 g (1 lb) jar ready-made tomato and herb sauce

2 garlic cloves, crushed

6 tablespoons finely chopped basil leaves

400 g (13 oz) can butter beans, drained and rinsed

salt and pepper

- Rub the butter into the plain flour until crumbs form. Stir in the chopped walnuts and grated cheese, season and set aside.

- Remove the carrots from the packs of prepared vegetables, roughly chop and boil for 2 minutes. Add the broccoli and cauliflower and cook for another minute, then drain.

- Meanwhile, heat the tomato and herb sauce in a large saucepan until bubbling.

- Stir in the garlic, basil, butter beans and blanched vegetables. Transfer to a medium-sized ovenproof dish and scatter over the crumble mixture. Bake in a preheated oven, 200°C (400°F), Gas Mark 6, for 15–20 minutes or until golden and bubbling.

1 Butter Bean and Walnut Pâté

Tip 2 x 400 g (13 oz) cans butter beans, drained, and the juice and finely grated zest of 1 lemon into a food processor with 1 crushed garlic clove, 4 tablespoons each of finely chopped basil and mint leaves, 50 g (2 oz) chopped walnuts, 8 tablespoons ready-made mayonnaise and 2 teaspoons Dijon mustard. Blend until fairly smooth and serve spread thickly on toasted sourdough bread with a salad.

2 Vegetable and Butter Bean Soup

Lightly fry 2 sliced cloves garlic and 1 chopped onion in 2 tablespoons olive oil for 1–2 minutes. Add 1 litre (1¾ pints) hot vegetable stock, 2 x 250 g (8 oz) packs prepared broccoli, cauliflower and carrots, 25 g (1 oz) chopped parsley and 2 x 400 g (13 oz) cans butter beans, drained, to the onion, and simmer for 15 minutes. Allow the soup to cool slightly, and then blend two-thirds using a hand-held blender. Return the blended soup to the vegetables along with 2 tablespoons tomato purée and mix well. Serve immediately, garnished with a little chopped parsley, if desired.

Quick Curried Egg Salad

Serves 4

8 hard-boiled eggs
4 tomatoes, cut into wedges
2 little gem lettuces, leaves
  separated
¼ cucumber, sliced
200 ml (7 fl oz) natural yogurt
1 tablespoon mild curry powder
3 tablespoons tomato purée
juice of 2 limes
6 tablespoons mayonnaise
thyme leaves, to garnish
salt and pepper

- Halve the eggs and place on a large platter with the tomatoes, lettuce leaves and cucumber.

- Mix the yogurt together with the curry powder, tomato purée, lime juice and mayonnaise. Season the dressing then pour it over the salad. Serve immediately, garnished with thyme leaves.

 Indian-Style Spicy Open Omelette

Heat 2 tablespoons of vegetable oil in a large ovenproof frying pan. Add 1 chopped onion, 1 chopped red chilli, 2 teaspoons cumin seeds, 1 teaspoon each of grated fresh root ginger and garlic, 1 teaspoon curry powder and 1 finely chopped tomato. Stir-fry for 3–4 minutes. Beat together 6 eggs and a small handful of finely chopped coriander. Season and pour over the vegetable mixture in the pan. Cook over a gentle heat for 8–10 minutes or until the base is starting to set, then place under a preheated hot grill for 3–4 minutes or until the top is set and lightly coloured. Remove and serve with warm naan bread and a salad.

 Egg and Tomato Curry Heat

2 tablespoons sunflower oil in a large, nonstick wok or frying pan. Add 1 tablespoon cumin seeds, 1 tablespoon black mustard seeds, 2 crushed garlic cloves, 2 dried red chillies and 10 fresh curry leaves and stir-fry for 30–40 seconds. Add 1 halved and thinly sliced onion and 2 tablespoons curry powder and stir in 200 g (7 oz) canned chopped tomatoes, 1 teaspoon sugar and 200 ml (7 fl oz) coconut cream. Bring to the boil, reduce the heat to medium–low, and cook for 8–10 minutes, stirring often. Add 8 shelled hard-boiled eggs and cook for 10–12 minutes until the sauce is thickened. Season with salt, garnish with coriander leaves and serve with warm naan bread.

Dessert in a Dash

Recipes listed by cooking time

10

Quick Mini Lemon Meringue Pies

Serves 4

4 individual sweet pastry cases

12 tablespoons lemon curd

1 egg white

50 g (2 oz) caster sugar

- Fill each pastry case with one-quarter of the lemon curd.

- In a large, clean bowl, whisk the egg white until it forms soft peaks and hold its shape. Gradually whisk in the sugar, a little at a time, until the mixture is thick and glossy.

- Pipe the meringue mixture in swirls over the lemon curd and bake on the top shelf of a preheated oven, 200°C (400°F), Gas Mark 6, for 5–6 minutes or until the meringue is just beginning to brown. Cool slightly and serve.

 Lemon Meringue and Blueberry Pots

Roughly crush 2 meringue nests and place in the base of 4 dessert bowls. Whip 200 ml (7 fl oz) double cream until softly peaked and then stir in 8 tablespoons lemon curd to create a marbled effect. Spoon this mixture over the crushed meringue and top each with 25 g (1 oz) blueberries.

 Luxurious Lemon Curd Tart

Sift 125 g (4 oz) plain flour into a mixing bowl. Add 50 g (2 oz) cool, diced butter and rub in until the mixture resembles breadcrumbs. Stir in 25 g (1 oz) icing sugar. Lightly beat 1 egg yolk with 1 tablespoon cold water, add to the flour mixture and mix with a round bladed knife. Gather together to form a soft dough. Roll out the dough and use to line a 23 cm (9 in) flan tin. Bake blind in a preheated oven, 180°C (350°F), Gas Mark 4, for 12–15 minutes, then remove the beans and baking paper and bake for a further 5–8 minutes or until lightly golden. Allow to cool. Spoon in 625 g (1¼ lb) lemon curd. Whisk 200 ml (7 fl oz) double cream and spread over the lemon curd. Cut into wedges and serve.

30 Baked Amaretto Figs

Serves 4

8–12 ripe figs (depending on their
  size; 2 or 3 per person)
4 large oranges, peeled and cut
  into thick slices
12 tablespoons amaretto liqueur
50 ml (2 fl oz) sweet white wine
4 tablespoons caster sugar
150 g (5 oz) mascarpone cheese,
  lightly beaten
4 tablespoons finely chopped
  pistachio nuts

- Trim the end of the stalks from each fig and cut in half.

- Place the orange slices in a shallow ovenproof dish and top
  with the fig halves.

- Mix together the amaretto, wine and sugar and pour
  over the fruit mixture. Cover loosely with foil and bake
  in a preheated oven, 200°C (400°F), Gas Mark 6, for
  10–12 minutes.

- Divide the mixture between 4 warmed plates and spoon
  over the syrup from the dish.

- Serve with a big dollop of mascarpone cheese and sprinkle
  over the pistachios.

 **Fig, Orange, Amaretto and Blue Cheese Salad** Thinly slice 12 ripe figs and place on a platter with 2 segmented oranges. Scatter over 100 g (3½ oz) diced creamy blue cheese. Make a dressing by whisking together the juice of 1 orange and 4 tablespoons amaretto and pour over the salad. Scatter over 50 g (2 oz) chopped pistachio nuts and serve.

 Grilled Fig and Amaretto Pots Thickly slice 12 figs and place on a lightly oiled grill rack. Sprinkle with 4 tablespoons caster sugar and place under a preheated hot grill for 4–5 minutes. Whisk together 200 ml (7 fl oz) double cream until softly peaked and stir in 4 tablespoons amaretto. Divide the figs between 4 dessert bowls and top with the amaretto cream. Sprinkle over 100 g (3½ oz) chopped pistachio nuts and serve immediately.

 Berry, Honey and Yogurt Pots

Serves 4

400 g (13 oz) frozen mixed
  berries, thawed
juice of 1 orange
6 tablespoons clear honey
400 ml (14 fl oz) vanilla yogurt
50 g (2 oz) granola

- Whizz half the berries with the orange juice and honey in a blender until fairly smooth.

- Transfer to a bowl and stir in the remaining berries.

- Divide one-third of the berry mixture between 4 dessert glasses or small bowls. Top with half the yogurt.

- Layer with half the remaining berry mixture and top with the remaining yogurt.

- Top with the remaining berry mixture and sprinkle over the granola just before serving.

 Berry and Orange Yogurt Smoothie

Peel and segment 2 large oranges and place the segments in a blender. Add 750 ml (1¼ pints) vanilla yogurt and 400 g (13 oz) frozen mixed berries. Spoon in 4 tablespoons clear honey and blend until thick and smooth. Pour into 4 chilled glasses and serve straight away.

 Berry and Yogurt Filo Tartlets

Cut 2 large sheets of filo pastry (in half and cut each half into 4 squares. Brush each square with melted butter. Stack 4 squares on top of each other and repeat with the remaining squares to create 4 stacks. Use to line 4 x 10 cm (4 in) deep tartlet tins. Bake the filo cases for 8–10 minutes in a preheated oven, 180°C (350°F), Gas Mark 4, until crispy and golden. Allow to cool and remove from the tins. To serve, place 2 tablespoons vanilla yogurt into each tartlet case and spoon over 200 g (7 oz) mixed berries. Dust with icing sugar and serve immediately.

30 Blackberry Crumble

Serves 4

750 g (1½ lb) blackberries
2 oranges, segmented
zest and juice of 1 orange
200 g (7 oz) butter
200 g (7 oz) plain flour
100 g (3½ oz) soft brown sugar
cream, ice cream or custard,
  to serve (optional)

- Mix the blackberries, orange segments and the orange zest and juice together in a bowl.

- In a separate bowl rub together the butter and flour with your fingertips until it resembles breadcrumbs and then stir in the sugar.

- Tip the blackberry mixture into a large pie dish and scatter over the crumble mixture to cover.

- Bake in a preheated oven, 220°C (425°F), Gas Mark 7, for 20–25 minutes until golden. Remove from the oven and serve warm with cream, ice cream or custard, if liked.

 Blackberry, Orange and Custard Pots

Divide 300 ml (½ pint) fresh custard between 4 dessert glasses. Whizz 200 g (7 oz) blackberries in a blender with 4 tablespoons caster sugar until smooth and spoon over the custard in the glasses. Peel and segment 2 large oranges and layer on top of the blackberry purée. Top each glass with a small scoop of vanilla ice cream and serve.

 Spiced Blackberry Chutney

In a large saucepan, stir together 500 g (1 lb) blackberries, 150 g (5 oz) caster sugar, 1 small sliced red onion, 1 tablespoon grated ginger and 1 tablespoon Dijon mustard. Cook, stirring continuously, over a medium heat until the blackberries burst. Season to taste. Add 100 ml (3½ fl oz) white wine vinegar and simmer uncovered for 10 minutes. Allow the mixture to cool slightly, transfer to a warm sterilized jar and seal immediately. Although a chutney, this goes well with warm scones and clotted cream.

20 Cherry and Vanilla Brûlée

Serves 4

300 g (10 oz) ripe cherries,
   stoned and roughly chopped
12 tablespoons caster sugar
50 g (2 oz) glace cherries,
   roughly chopped
4 tablespoons kirsch or
   cherry liqueur
400 ml (14 fl oz) vanilla yogurt

· Mix the fresh cherries in a bowl with the half the sugar, and the chopped glace cherries and kirsch.

· Spoon the cherry mixture into 4 glass ramekins and top with the yogurt.

· Sprinkle the remaining caster sugar over the yogurt and use a blow-torch (or place the ramekins under a preheated hot grill for 2–3 minutes) to caramelize the tops. Serve immediately.

---

10 Cherry and Raspberry Brûlée

Place a mixture of 300 g (10 oz) stoned cherries and 300 g (10 oz) raspberries in a shallow ovenproof dish. Spoon over 400 ml (14 fl oz) fresh ready-made custard and sprinkle over 4 tablespoons caster sugar. Cook under a preheated medium-high grill for 4–5 minutes or until lightly browned and bubbling. Serve immediately.

30 White Chocolate, Vanilla and Cherry Cookies

Beat 200 g (7 oz) unsalted butter, 75 g (3 oz) muscovado sugar, 75 g (3 oz) golden caster sugar, 1–2 drops of vanilla extract and 1 egg until smooth, then mix in 250 g (8 oz) self-raising flour, 100 g (3½ oz) white chocolate chips, 75 g (3 oz) chopped glacé cherries and ½ teaspoon salt. Spoon large rough blobs on to nonstick baking sheets – the mixture makes about 20. Give each blob plenty of space as the cookies 'grow' substantially as they bake. Bake in a preheated oven, 190°C (375°F), Gas Mark 5, for 12–14 minutes until just golden, but still pale and soft in the middle. Allow to cool on the baking sheets for 5 minutes before lifting on to wire racks and then leave to cool completely.

30 Chocolate Fondant Puddings

Serves 4

150 g (5 oz) butter, cubed, plus
 extra for greasing
25 g (1 oz) cocoa powder
200 g (7 oz) dark chocolate
 (at least 70 per cent cocoa
 solids), in pieces
2 eggs, plus 2 egg yolks
125 g (4 oz) golden caster sugar
25 g (1 oz) plain flour
crème fraîche, to serve

- Grease 4 x 200 ml (7 fl oz) pudding moulds or ramekins and dust with half the cocoa powder. Place on a baking sheet.

- Put the chocolate and butter in a heatproof bowl over a pan of just-simmering water. Stir occasionally until melted, smooth and glossy. Set aside to cool.

- Meanwhile, beat the eggs, egg yolks and sugar in a bowl for 5 minutes until thick and foamy.

- Whisk the cooled chocolate mixture into the egg mixture, then sift in the flour and remaining cocoa and fold in.

- Divide the mixture between the moulds or ramekins. Bake the puddings in a preheated oven, 180°C (350°F), Gas Mark 4, for 14–16 minutes, or until the outsides are set but the insides are still soft. Hold each mould with a cloth, then carefully run a sharp knife around each pudding and invert on to a warmed plate. Alternatively, serve in the ramekins if using. Accompany with a scoop of cold crème fraîche.

 Chocolate and Banana Pancakes Melt 200 g (7 oz) dark chocolate in a small saucepan. Place 4 ready-made pancakes on to 4 serving plates and slice a banana into the centre of each one. Drizzle over the melted chocolate and serve.

 Chocolate and Honeycomb Mousse Pots Break 150 g (5 oz) milk chocolate into pieces and melt gently in a small saucepan, then stir in 2 x 40 g (1½ oz) bars of roughly broken honeycomb chocolate bars. Gently stir 300 ml (½ pint) double cream into 250 g (8 oz) mascarpone till combined and then stir in the chocolate mixture to create a marbled effect. Spoon into small glasses or cups and dust with cocoa and serve.

30 Spiced Drop Scones with Ice Cream and Chocolate Sauce

Serves 4

250 g (8 oz) self-raising flour
1 teaspoon ground cinnamon
1 teaspoon allspice
50 g (2 oz) golden caster sugar
1 egg
300 ml (½ pint) milk
sunflower oil, for shallow-frying

To serve

4 scoops vanilla ice cream
8 tablespoons ready-made
  chocolate sauce

- Place the flour, cinnamon, allspice and sugar in bowl and make a well in the centre.

- Beat the egg and pour into the centre of the flour mixture.

- Gradually add the milk, beating well until smooth.

- Heat a little oil in a heavy-based frying pan or griddle until moderately hot.

- Working in batches, drop large tablespoons of the mixture into the pan and cook for 1–2 minutes until bubbles appear on the surface and the underneath is golden brown. Turn the drop scone over and cook the other side for 1–2 minutes. Place a tea towel or kitchen paper between each scone and keep warm on a preheated plate in a preheated oven, 150°C (300°F), Gas Mark 2. Repeat until all the batter has been used.

- Serve 3 drop scones per person with scoops of vanilla ice cream and drizzle over the chocolate sauce.

 Mixed Spiced Biscuits

Cream 100 g (3½ oz) softened butter with 75 g (3 oz) light muscovado sugar, 1 teaspoon ground cinnamon and ¼ teaspoon all-spice, beat in 1 egg and 175 g (6 oz) sieved self-raising flour. Drop spoonfuls of the mixture on to a baking sheet lined with baking parchment and bake in a preheated oven, 180°C (350°F), Gas Mark 4, for 8–10 minutes. Remove and allow to cool on racks.

 Ricotta Pancakes with Chocolate Sauce Sift 75 g (3 oz) self-raising flour, 1 teaspoon ground cinnamon, ½ teaspoon salt and 25 g (1 oz) caster sugar together into a large bowl. Whisk 2 egg yolks, reserving the egg whites, 90 ml (6 tablespoons) buttermilk and 40 g (1½ oz) melted butter and lightly mix into the dry ingredients. Carefully fold in 100 g (3½ oz) ricotta. Whisk the reserved egg whites until softly peaked, then carefully fold them into the batter one-third at a time. Heat a little butter in a large ovenproof frying pan, then add about 3 tablespoons of batter for each pancake, spaced apart. Put the pan into a preheated oven, 160°C (325°F), Gas Mark 3, for 4 minutes, then remove and flip the pancakes. Return to the oven for a further 4 minutes or until the pancakes feel firm to the touch. Place a pancake on each plate and drizzle over some ready-made chocolate sauce and serve with a dollop of crème fraîche on the side.

30 Blueberry Pancakes

Serves 4

250 ml (8 fl oz) milk
2 eggs
100 g (3½ oz) caster sugar
75 g (3 oz) butter, melted, plus
    extra for greasing
1 teaspoon baking powder
pinch of salt
250 g (8 oz) plain flour
100 g (3½ oz) blueberries, plus
    extra to serve
maple syrup or clear honey,
    to serve

- Whisk together the milk, eggs, sugar and melted butter in a large bowl. Whisk in the baking powder and salt, add half the flour and whisk well until all the ingredients are incorporated, then whisk in the remaining flour. Stir in the blueberries to mix well.

- Heat a large, nonstick pan over a medium-high heat. Grease the base of the pan with a little melted butter using kitchen paper. Lower the heat to medium. Spoon in large tablespoons of the batter until the pan is full, allowing a little space between each pancake. Add extra butter for frying if required.

- Cook for 1–2 minutes on each side or until golden brown, then set aside and keep warm. Continue until all the batter is used.

- Divide the pancakes between 4 plates that have been warmed in a preheated oven, 150°C (300°F), Gas Mark 2, and drizzle over a little maple syrup or honey. Serve immediately, with extra blueberries.

 Blueberry Cheesecake Pots
Crush 4 ginger biscuits and place in the base of 4 individual dessert glasses. Mix together 250 g (8 oz) mascarpone, 4 tablespoons double cream, 4 tablespoons icing sugar and the juice and grated zest of 1 lemon. Spoon over the biscuit base, top with 150 g (5 oz) blueberries and serve.

 Brioche French Toast with Blueberry Compote Make the compote by gently heating 100 g (3½ oz) blueberries in a saucepan with 2 tablespoons caster sugar and a squeeze of lemon juice. When the blueberries start to burst and release their juices simmer for 2–3 minutes until they reach a jam-like consistency. Meanwhile, make the French toast. In a wide bowl, mix together 2 eggs, 4 tablespoons milk, 1 tablespoon caster sugar and a few drops of vanilla extract and stir until the sugar has dissolved. Dip 4 thick slices of brioche in the egg mix to thoroughly coat. Heat a little butter in a large frying pan and fry the brioche until golden brown on both sides. Serve the French toast with a scoop of vanilla ice cream and the blueberry compote.

30 French Toast with Blueberries and Redcurrants

Serves 4

3 eggs
100 ml (3½ fl oz) milk
50 ml (2 fl oz) double cream
100 g (3½ oz) caster sugar
2 teaspoons ground cinnamon
6 slices thick white bread
400 g (13 oz) mixed blueberries
  and redcurrants
2 tablespoons water
75 g (3 oz) butter
crème fraîche, to serve

- In a large bowl, whisk together the eggs, milk, cream, half the sugar and a pinch of the cinnamon.

- Soak the bread in the egg mixture for a couple of minutes.

- In a frying pan, combine the remaining cinnamon with the remaining caster sugar and toss the berries in the mixture until they are well coated. Add the water and heat the mixture over a medium heat for 3–4 minutes. Remove from the heat and keep warm.

- In a separate large nonstick frying pan, melt half the butter. Carefully drain 3 slices of bread and fry for 2–3 minutes on each side, or until golden-brown. Repeat with the remaining butter and the remaining 3 slices of bread. Drain the toast on kitchen paper, cut each in half diagonally, and arrange the slices on serving plates that have been warmed in a preheated oven, 150°C (300°F), Gas Mark 2.

- Spoon the berry mixture around and serve immediately with a dollop of crème fraîche.

 Grilled Berry and Brioche Toast

Lightly toast 4 thick slices of brioche. Whip 50 ml (2 fl oz) double cream with 4 tablespoons caster sugar until stiff and spread on top of the toasted brioche slices. Spoon over 200 g (7 oz) mixed blueberries and redcurrants, dust with icing sugar and serve.

 Crunchy Creamy Berry Sundaes

Whisk 400 ml (14 fl oz) double cream in a bowl. Roughly break 2 meringue nests into the cream and add 100 g (3½ oz) redcurrants and 200 g (7 oz) blueberries. Gently fold together so that the fruit is marbled through the cream. Place a large scoop of vanilla ice cream in the bottom of 4 sundae glasses and top with spoonfuls of the berry cream and dust with icing sugar.

 Instant Summer Berry Sorbet

Serves 4

300 g (10 oz) frozen summer
   berries
400 ml (14 fl oz) raspberry yogurt
6 tablespoons icing sugar

- Tip the frozen berries, yogurt and sugar into a food processor or blender. Whizz until blended.

- Scrape the mixture from the sides and blend again.

- Spoon into chilled glasses or bowls and serve immediately.

2 **Frozen Berries with White and Dark Hot Chocolate Sauce**

Divide 400 g (13 oz) frozen mixed berries between 4 chilled serving plates or shallow bowls. Melt 100 g (3½ oz) dark chocolate and 100 g (3½ oz) white chocolate in 2 separate small pans. Whisk 150 ml (¼ pint) double cream until softly peaked. When ready to serve, drizzle the hot chocolate sauces over the frozen berries and serve immediately with a dollop of the whipped cream.

3 **Mini Mixed Berry Clafoutis**

Lightly grease 4 x 200 ml (7 fl oz) ramekins and divide 300 g (10 oz) thawed frozen mixed berries between them. Whisk 125 g (4 oz) cream cheese with 150 g (5 oz) caster sugar and 50 g (2 oz) plain flour until smooth. Whisk in a few drops of vanilla extract, 3 eggs and 6 tablespoons milk. Pour evenly over the berries and bake in a preheated oven, 200°C (400°F), Gas Mark 6, for 20 minutes or until golden-brown. Dust with icing sugar and serve with raspberry yogurt.

Mango and Custard Fools

Serves 4

4 firm, ripe, sweet mangoes
200 ml (7 fl oz) canned mango
  purée
50 g (2 oz) caster sugar
150 ml (¼ pint) double cream
¼ teaspoon crushed cardamom
  seeds, plus extra to decorate
200 ml (7 fl oz) ready-made fresh
  custard

- Peel and stone the mango and cut the flesh into small bite-sized cubes. Place three-quarters of the mango in to a blender along with the mango purée and sugar and blend until smooth.

- Lightly whisk the cream with the cardamom seeds until softly peaked and gently fold in the custard. Lightly fold one-quarter of the mango mixture into the custard mixture to give a marbled effect.

- Divide half the remaining mango cubes between 4 individual serving glasses and top with half the fool. Layer over half the remaining mango mixture.

- Decorate with the remaining mango cubes and a sprinkling of crushed cardamom seeds and chill until ready to serve.

10 Mango and Cardamom Lassi

Peel and stone 3 ripe mangoes and place the flesh in a blender with 4 tablespoons of clear honey, 500 ml (17 fl oz) natural yogurt and 1 teaspoon crushed cardamom seeds. Whizz until smooth, pour into 4 tall, ice-filled glasses and serve.

30 Fragrant Mango Tartlets

Cut a sheet of ready-rolled puff pastry in half lengthways, then cut each half into 4 evenly sized rectangles. Place on a baking sheet lined with baking parchment. Brush with 2 tablespoons milk and sprinkle with 1 tablespoon demerara sugar. Peel, stone and thinly slice 2 ripe mangoes. Arrange the slices on the pastry rectangles then drizzle over 2 tablespoons clear honey and scatter over 1 teaspoon crushed cardamom seeds. Bake in a preheated oven, 200 °C (400 °F), Gas Mark 6, for 15–20 minutes until puffed up and golden. Serve with ready-made fresh custard.

10 Mixed Berry Eton Mess

Serves 4

400 g (13 oz) mixed berries (such as blackberries, raspberries, blueberries), plus extra to decorate

400 ml (14 fl oz) strawberry yogurt

300 ml (½ pint) crème fraîche

4 tablespoons icing sugar

4 meringue nests, roughly crushed

- Place half the berries in a blender and blend until smooth. Transfer to a bowl with the strawberry yogurt and stir to mix well.

- Place the remaining berries in a bowl and mix in the crème fraîche and icing sugar. Add this mixture to the berry and yogurt mixture and swirl through to create a marbled effect.

- Fold in the crushed meringue and spoon into 4 chilled dessert glasses.

- Serve immediately, decorated with berries.

 Layered Summer Berry and Yogurt Compote Heat 500 g (1 lb) mixed summer berries in a saucepan with 50 g (2 oz) caster sugar and a few drops of vanilla extract for 4–5 minutes or until just softened and bursting. Remove from the heat and set aside to cool. Spoon half the mixture into 4 dessert glasses or bowls. Top first with 200 ml (7 fl oz) strawberry yogurt and then with the remaining berry mixture. Crumble over 2 meringue nests and serve at room temperature or chilled.

 Summer Berry Trifles Gently cook 200 g (7 oz) each raspberries, blueberries and blackberries, 50 g (2 oz) caster sugar and 2 tablespoons water in a small pan for 2–3 minutes until the fruit is just soft. Allow to cool. Break 4 trifle sponges into small pieces and use to line 4 individual dessert bowls or glasses. Spoon over the berry mixture followed by 200 ml (7 fl oz) fresh vanilla custard. Top each with a spoonful of crème fraîche and chill until ready to serve.

30 Peach and Raspberry Cheesecake Pots

Serves 4

150 g (5 oz) mascarpone cheese

finely grated zest and juice of
  1 lemon

75 g (3 oz) caster sugar, plus
  1 tablespoon

150 ml (5 fl oz) double cream

400 g (13 oz) fresh raspberries

4 fresh ripe peaches

- Beat the mascarpone with the lemon zest and juice and sugar until smooth. Whisk the cream until it just holds its shape then fold into the cheese mixture.

- Pulse one-quarter of the raspberries in a food processor or blender with the remaining 1 tablespoon caster sugar, for 1–2 minutes or until smooth. Transfer to a bowl. Fold in the remaining berries.

- Peel, stone and cut the peaches into thick slices and arrange half the slices in the base of 4 dessert glasses or bowls.

- Spoon half the cheese mixture over the peaches and then top with the raspberry mixture. Continue to layer, finishing off with the raspberry mixture. Chill until ready to serve.

10 Peach and Raspberry Salad with Lemon Mascarpone

Arrange slices of peaches from 4 ripe, peeled and stoned peaches on a serving platter with 200g (7 oz) raspberries. Whisk together 100 g (3½ oz) mascarpone with 75 ml (3 fl oz) double cream, the juice and finely grated zest of ½ lemon and 50 g (2 oz) caster sugar. Serve the fruit salad with a generous dollop of the cream mixture.

20 Peach and Raspberry Zabaglione

Place slices from 3 ripe, peeled and stoned peaches into a large frying pan over a medium-high heat and sprinkle with 2 tablespoons caster sugar and 3 tablespoons Marsala. Fry for 2–3 minutes, until just tender. Spoon into 4 dessert glasses, top with 100 g (3½ oz) raspberries and set aside. Whisk 4 egg yolks and 75 g (3 oz) caster sugar in a stainless steel or heatproof glass bowl for 5 minutes, until thick and pale yellow. Place the bowl over a pan of barely simmering water and whisk for 15 minutes, drizzling in 150 ml (¼ pint) Marsala, until the mixture almost triples in volume and is light, foamy and holding soft peaks. Take care not to over-heat the mixture or it will begin to cook. Spoon on top of the peaches and raspberries and serve while still warm.

30 Rhubarb, Orange and Stem Ginger Pots

Serves 4

300 g (10 oz) rhubarb

2 balls of stem ginger in syrup
(from a jar), drained and finely
chopped

50 g (2 oz) caster sugar

2 cloves

1 cinnamon stick

2 oranges, 1 juiced and
1 peeled and segmented

50 g (2 oz) mascarpone cheese

100 ml (3½ fl oz) natural yogurt

- Cut the rhubarb into bite-sized pieces and place in a saucepan with half the ginger, the sugar, cloves, cinnamon stick and the orange juice.

- Place over a high heat and when bubbling, reduce the heat, cover with a lid and simmer, stirring occasionally, for 4–5 minutes or until just tender. Discard the cloves and cinnamon and allow to cool.

- Divide the orange segments between 4 dessert glasses. Whisk together the mascarpone and yogurt until smooth and then layer alternately with the rhubarb and the mascarpone mixture in the glasses.

- Chill until ready to serve, topping each with the remaining chopped ginger.

 Stewed Rhubarb and Ginger

Compote Place 500 g (1 lb) chopped rhubarb in a saucepan with 4 tablespoons roughly chopped stem ginger, juice and finely grated zest of 1 orange and 100 g (3½ oz) caster sugar and bring to the boil. Cook for 3–4 minutes or until the rhubarb has softened. Serve warm, spooned over scoops of vanilla ice cream.

 Rhubarb and Stem Ginger Crumbles

Grease 4 x 300 ml (½ pint) ramekins or ovenproof dishes. Place 400 g (13 oz) rhubarb chopped into 2.5 cm (1 in) pieces into the ramekins. Add 2 tablespoons finely chopped stem ginger with a little of the syrup from the jar and sprinkle over 1 teaspoon caster sugar. Divide 200 ml (7 fl oz) fresh ready-made custard between the ramekins and set aside. Rub together 100 g (3½ oz) plain flour with 75 g (3 oz) butter until it resembles breadcrumbs. Stir in 50 g (2 oz) caster sugar and sprinkle over the custard. Bake in a preheated oven, 180°C (350°F), Gas Mark 4, for 15 minutes, or until bubbling and golden.

Chocolate Fondue with a Selection of Dippers

Serves 4

400 g (13 oz) dark chocolate, broken into small pieces
25 g (1 oz) unsalted butter
150 ml (¼ pint) double cream
50 ml (2 fl oz) milk
strawberries and marshmallows, for dipping

- In a small saucepan gently heat the chocolate, butter, cream and milk, stirring occasionally, until the chocolate is melted and the sauce is glossy and smooth. Transfer to a warmed bowl or fondue pot.

- Thread 1 or 2 strawberries and marshmallows on to skewers, dip into the dark chocolate fondue and eat straight away.

 Chocolate-Dipped Strawberries

Melt 200 g (7 oz) dark chocolate in a small saucepan. Line a tray with baking parchment. Dip 20 ripe strawberries in the chocolate to coat two-thirds of the way up. Place on the tray and chill in the refrigerator until set and ready to serve.

 Chocolate-Stuffed Croissants with Strawberries Line a baking sheet with baking parchment. Chop a 200 g (7 oz) bar of dark chocolate into small squares. Split open 4 croissants and tuck the chocolate squares inside each one. Place the croissants on the baking sheet and bake in a preheated oven, 160 °C (325 °F), Gas Mark 3, for 8–10 minutes or until the chocolate melts and the croissants are warmed through. Dust the croissants with icing sugar and serve with scoops of vanilla ice cream and strawberries.

Spiced Caramelized Pineapple with Rum

Serves 4

50 g (2 oz) butter

4 tablespoons caster sugar

625 g (1¼ lb) pineapple flesh, cut into bite-sized pieces

2–3 star anise

1 cinnamon stick

2–3 tablespoons of dark rum

cream or ice cream, to serve

· Heat the butter in a large frying pan until it begins to foam.

· Add the sugar, pineapple, star anise and cinnamon stick and cook for 5–6 minutes over a high heat, stirring continuously, until the sugar mixture starts to caramelize.

· Pour in the rum and stir to mix well. Cook for a further 1–2 minutes, then remove from the heat and serve immediately with a dollop of cream or ice cream.

 Pineapple Skewers with Spiced Sugar Sprinkle Using a pestle and mortar grind together 50 g (2 oz) caster sugar, 1 teaspoon ground cinnamon and 1 teaspoon crushed star anise. Thread 500 g (1 lb) fresh pineapple cubes on to 8 wooden skewers. Sprinkle with the spiced sugar and serve with a dollop of cream.

 Spiced Rum-Poached Pineapple Place 625 g (1¼ lb) cubed fresh pineapple into a saucepan with 400 ml (14 fl oz) water, 6 tablespoons dark rum, 1 cinnamon stick, 2 star anise, 2 cloves and 150 g (5 oz) caster sugar and bring to the boil. Reduce the heat to low and cook gently for 12–15 minutes. Remove from the heat, discard the spices and allow to cool. Serve warm or cold in bowls with the poaching liquid and a dollop of cream or scoop of ice cream.

Fresh Berry Tart

Serves 4

1 x 375 g (12 oz) block puff pastry
200 ml (7 fl oz) double cream
75 ml (3 fl oz) ready-made fresh vanilla custard
1 tablespoon kirsch or cherry liqueur
300 g (10 oz) blackberries
200 g (7 oz) raspberries
200 g (7 oz) blueberries
icing sugar, to dust

- On a floured surface, thinly roll out the pastry to fit a 23 cm (9 in) tart tin. Trim the edges with a sharp knife and place on a baking sheet.

- Using the tip of a knife, score the pastry 1.5 cm (¾ in) from the edge to form a border.

- Bake the pastry case in a preheated oven, 220°C (425°F), Gas Mark 7, for 12–15 minutes or until puffed up and golden.

- Remove from the oven and press the base of the pastry down to create a shell with raised sides. Set aside to cool.

- Whisk the cream until stiff and then mix in the custard and kirsch or liqueur. Spoon into the centre of the cooled pastry base.

- Arrange the fruit attractively on the cream mixture, dust with icing sugar and serve immediately.

---

1 **Mixed Berries, Kirsch and Custard Pots** Mix together 200 g (7 oz) each blackberries, raspberries and blueberries in a bowl with 4 tablespoons caster sugar and 2 tablespoons kirsch. Spoon into 4 deep individual ramekins or dessert bowls. Spoon over 400 ml (14 fl oz) fresh ready-made custard, dust with cocoa powder and serve immediately.

2 **Berry and Lemon Syllabubs** Crumble 4 shortbread biscuits into the bottom of 4 sundae glasses. Drizzle 1 tablespoon kirsch into each glass. Whisk 250 ml (8 fl oz) double cream in a bowl and add 4 tablespoons icing sugar. Add 8 tablespoons lemon curd and 200 g (7 oz) lightly crushed mixed fresh berries and lightly fold to create a marbled effect. Spoon the cream mixture into the glasses. Top with 2 tablespoons flaked almonds and a sprig of mint and serve.

10 Luscious Victoria and Strawberry Sponge

Serves 4

1 ready-made round sponge cake (about 15 cm/6 in diameter)
150 g (5 oz) double cream
200 g (7 oz) small strawberries, halved
8 tablespoons good-quality strawberry jam
icing sugar, to dust

- Halve the sponge cake horizontally and place the base on a serving plate.

- Whip the cream until softly peaked and spread over the cut side of the base with a palette knife.

- Mix together the strawberries and jam and spoon carefully over the cream.

- Top with the sponge lid, press down lightly and dust the top with icing sugar. Cut into thick slices and serve immediately.

---

 2 Indian Strawberry Shrikhand

Hull and roughly chop 300 g (10 oz) strawberries and place in a bowl with 2 tablespoons rosewater and 6 tablespoons icing sugar. Line 4 dessert bowls with a thick slice of sponge cake and spoon over the strawberry mixture. Whisk together 400 g (13 oz) thick Greek yogurt with 8 tablespoons strawberry jam and spoon over the strawberry mixture. Chill until ready to serve.

 3 Mini Victoria Sponge Cakes

Grease and line the bases of 8 individual, springform cake tins (about 10 cm/4 in diameter) and place on a large baking tray. Beat 150 g (5 oz) butter with 150 g (5 oz) caster sugar in a large bowl until pale and fluffy. In a separate bowl, beat 3 eggs with a few drops of vanilla extract, then gradually beat into the butter mixture. Sift over 150 g (5 oz) self-raising flour and gently fold in until just combined.

Divide evenly between the prepared cake tins, smoothing the surface. Bake in a preheated oven, 180°C (350°F), Gas Mark 4, for 20 minutes or until risen and golden. Cool in the tin, then turn out on to a wire rack and cool. Meanwhile, lightly whip 300 ml (½ pint) double cream to soft peaks and spread over 4 of the cooled sponge bases. Top with 2 tablespoons strawberry jam and sandwich with the remaining sponge discs. Dust each with icing sugar to serve.

30 Tropical Fruit Trifles

Serves 4

1 large passionfruit

2 tablespoons icing sugar
(or to taste)

juice of 1 orange

4 kiwi fruits

1 mango

10–12 seedless green and red
grapes

4 thick slices sponge cake

400 ml (14 fl oz) ready-made
fresh custard

For the topping

100 ml (3½ fl oz) double cream,
softly whipped

julienned orange zest,
to decorate

- Prepare the fruit by scraping the seeds from a passionfruit into a large mixing bowl. Mix in the icing sugar and orange juice.

- Peel and finely dice the kiwi fruits. Peel the mango, then cut the flesh into 1 cm (½ in) dice.

- Add the diced fruit to the passionfruit mixture with the grapes. Chill until ready to serve.

- To assemble the trifles, take 4 dessert bowls or glasses and arrange the cake and fruit salad in the base. Pour the custard over the top.

- Place a dollop of whipped cream on top of the custard and serve decorated with the orange zest.

10 Tropical Fruit Salad
Place 1 cubed mango in a bowl with 300 g (10 oz) cubed pineapple, 4 peeled and cubed kiwi fruit and 200 g (7 oz) seedless green and red grapes. Add the juice of 1 orange and 6 tablespoons icing sugar and toss to mix well. Serve with ice cream.

20 Tropical Fruit and Custard Tart
Line the base of a 20 cm (8 in) ready-made sweet shortcrust pastry case with 200 ml (7 fl oz) ready-made fresh custard. Peel, halve and stone 2 ripe mangoes and cut into thin slices. Peel 2 kiwi fruits and cut into thin slices. Arrange the mango and kiwi slices over the custard in the pastry case with 100 g (3½ oz) of halved green and red seedless grapes. Dust with icing sugar and serve with whipped cream.

20 Watermelon, Lime and Grenadine Squares

Serves 4

4 tablespoons grenadine
50 g (2 oz) caster sugar
juice and finely grated zest
of 1 lime, plus extra lime zest
to decorate
100 ml (3½ fl oz) water
1 small–medium watermelon

- Place the grenadine, sugar and lime juice and zest with the measured water in a small saucepan and bring to the boil. Reduce the heat and cook gently for 6–8 minutes until thick and syrupy. Remove from the heat and allow to cool.

- Meanwhile halve the watermelon and, using a sharp knife, slice the rind from the bottom of each half.

- Lay the halves on a cutting board and, working from top to bottom, trim the rind from the watermelon flesh in 4 cuts, creating 2 large squares.

- Cut each square of watermelon into equal bite-sized squares and place on a serving platter to form a neat large square (made up of the bite-sized squares).

- Drizzle over the cooled grenadine syrup, scatter over the lime zest and serve immediately.

 Iced Watermelon, Lime and Grenadine Coolers Whizz the flesh of ½ a watermelon in a blender with 4 tablespoons grenadine, 4 tablespoons caster sugar, 4 tablespoons chopped mint leaves and the juice and finely grated zest of 1 lime. Fill 4 tall glasses with crushed ice, pour over the watermelon mixture and serve immediately.

 Watermelon Skewers with Lime and Mint Syrup Heat 200 g (7 oz) caster sugar in a saucepan with 150 ml (¼ pint) water and bring to the boil. Reduce the heat and cook gently for 15–20 minutes until the sugar has dissolved and the mixture has thickened. Remove from the heat and stir in the juice and finely grated zest of 1 lime and 4 tablespoons finely chopped mint leaves. Allow to cool. Meanwhile, cut the flesh from ½ watermelon into bite-sized cubes and thread on to 8 wooden skewers. Place on a shallow platter and pour over the lime syrup. Serve at room temperature or chilled.

 # Blackberry, Cinnamon and Apple Cranachan

Serves 4

4 teaspoons porridge oats
8 teaspoons caster sugar
250 g (8 oz) vanilla yogurt
½ teaspoon ground cinnamon
1 tablespoon whisky
400 g (13 oz) blackberries,
   plus extra for decoration
2 tablespoons butter
1 dessert apple, peeled, cored
   and coarsely grated

- Place a small frying pan over a medium high heat. Add the oats and cook for 1 minute, then add 3 teaspoons of the sugar.

- Dry-fry, stirring for 2–3 minutes, or until the oats are lightly browned, then tip on to a piece of nonstick baking paper and leave to cool. Mix together the yogurt, cinnamon, 1 teaspoon of the sugar and the whisky.

- Stir in the blackberries, crushing them slightly.

- Heat a nonstick pan over a high heat, add the butter and sauté the apple for 3–4 minutes. When the apple begins to soften, add the remaining sugar and cook until lightly browned. Set aside to cool.

- Layer the blackberry mixture with the apple in 4 dessert glasses. Top with blackberries, sprinkle over the oat mixture and serve.

 Warm Blackberry and Cinnamon Compote Heat 625 g (1¼ lb) blackberries with 1 teaspoon ground cinnamon, 4 tablespoons caster sugar and a squeeze of lemon juice in a saucepan and bring to the boil. Cook for 5–6 minutes or until the berries have broken down and the mixture has thickened. Serve warm over scoops of ice cream or with vanilla yogurt.

Individual Crunchy Blackberry and Apple Crumbles Peel, core and chop 625 g (1¼ lb) Bramley apples into small chunks. Squeeze the juice of ½ lemon over the apple chunks and mix well. In 4 x 300 ml (½ pint) ramekins or ovenproof dishes, layer the apples with 200 g (7 oz) blackberries and 175 g (6 oz) demerara sugar. For the crumble topping, rub 250 g (8 oz) butter into 250 g (8 oz) plain flour in a large bowl until it resembles breadcrumbs. Mix in 125 g (4 oz) muesli and 50 g (2 oz) soft brown sugar and stir. Sprinkle the crumble topping evenly over the fruit. Bake in a preheated oven, 200°C (400°F), Gas Mark 6, for 20 minutes or until the fruit is cooked and bubbling juices seep through the topping. Cool for a few minutes and then serve with custard or fresh cream.

30 Chocolate and Raspberry Roulade

Serves 4

butter, for greasing
100 g (3½ oz) plain chocolate,
  broken into squares
4 large eggs, separated
100 g (3½ oz) caster sugar
50 g (2 oz) self-raising flour,
  sifted
300 ml (½ pint) double cream
300 g (10 oz) raspberries, plus
  extra to decorate
cocoa powder, for dusting

- Grease and line a 30 x 23 cm (12 x 9 in) Swiss roll tin with nonstick baking paper.

- Melt the chocolate in a heatproof bowl over a pan of barely simmering water.

- In a large bowl, beat the egg yolks and sugar until pale and creamy. Stir in the chocolate and flour.

- Using a clean whisk, beat the egg whites in a separate bowl until stiff peaks form. Carefully fold the whites into the chocolate mixture until well combined.

- Tip the sponge mixture into the prepared tin and shake to level it. Bake in a preheated oven, 180°C (350°F), Gas Mark 4, for 15–20 minutes, or until the sponge is slightly risen and just firm to the touch.

- Carefully invert the sponge on to nonstick baking paper. Peel the paper from the base of the roulade and discard. Roll up in the fresh paper.

- Whip the cream and gently fold in the raspberries.

- Unroll the roulade and spread over the raspberry cream, leaving a small gap around the edge. Re-roll the roulade (don't worry about any cracks). Dust with the cocoa powder, decorate with raspberries, and serve immediately.

 Chocolate and Raspberry Squares Whip 50 ml (2 fl oz) cream and spread over 4 ready-made chocolate brownies. Top each with 10–12 raspberries, dust with icing sugar and serve immediately.

 Melting Chocolate Soufflés with Raspberries Grease 4 medium ramekins. Melt 200 g (7 oz) dark chocolate with 150 g (5 oz) butter in a bowl over simmering water or in a microwave. Beat 4 eggs with 150 g (5 oz) caster sugar until light and fluffy and then sift in 100 g (3½ oz) plain flour. Fold in the chocolate mixture. Divide between the ramekins and bake in a preheated oven, 180°C (350°F), Gas Mark 4, for 8–12 minutes. The soufflés should rise and form a firm crust but should still be slightly runny in the middle. Serve each with a handful of raspberries and cream.

30 Lime, Banana and Coconut Fritters

Serves 4

juice of 2 limes
6 tablespoons caster sugar
4 bananas, sliced into three or
    four pieces
200 g (7 oz) cornflour
100 g (3½ oz) self-raising flour
3 tablespoons dessicated coconut
3 large egg yolks
75 ml (3 fl oz) chilled soda or
    sparkling water
vegetable oil, for deep-frying
icing sugar, for dusting
clear honey, for drizzling

· Mix together the lime juice and caster sugar in a bowl. Add the bananas, stir well to coat and leave for 5 minutes.

· Roll the bananas in half the cornflour until well coated and set aside. Sieve the remaining cornflour and self-raising flour into a bowl. Add the coconut.

· Whisk together the egg yolks and soda or sparkling water in a clean bowl. Add the flour mixture and whisk again, until the mixture forms a thick batter.

· Fill a deep medium-sized saucepan one-quarter full of vegetable oil. Heat the oil to 180°C (350°F) or until a cube of bread turns golden in 10–15 seconds.

· Dip the bananas into the batter and carefully place into the hot vegetable oil to deep-fry for 1–2 minutes, in batches, until golden brown. Carefully remove with a slotted spoon and drain on to kitchen paper. Keep warm on a plate in a preheated oven, 150°C (300°F), Gas Mark 2.

· Serve immediately, dusted with icing sugar and drizzled with honey.

10 Boozy Strawberries with Lime and Coconut

In a large bowl, mix together 2 tablespoons caster sugar, 2 tablespoons Cointreau or orange liqueur and the juice of ½ lime. Stir in 200 g (7 oz) freshly grated coconut and 200 g (7 oz) chopped strawberries. Toss to mix well and serve.

20 Lime and Coconut Rice Pudding

Heat 200 ml (7 fl oz) coconut cream and 100 ml (3½ fl oz) coconut milk in a saucepan with 150 g (5 oz) caster sugar and the finely grated zest of 2 limes. Bring to the boil and add 250 g (8 oz) cooked basmati rice. Cook for 4–5 minutes or until thickened. Ladle into bowls and serve decorated with mint sprigs.

30 Individual Mixed Berry Swirl Cheesecakes

Serves 4

25 g (1 oz) butter
1 tablespoon golden syrup
125 g (4 oz) bourbon biscuits

For the filling

200 g (7 oz) mixed summer
   berries, plus extra to decorate
175 g (6 oz) cream cheese
100 g (3½ oz) caster sugar
juice and grated zest of 1 lemon
½ teaspoon vanilla extract
   or essence
2 tablespoons water
½ sachet powdered vegetarian
   gelatine
250 ml (8 fl oz) double cream
mint leaves, to decorate

- Place the butter and golden syrup in a saucepan and melt over a medium heat. Whizz the biscuits into crumbs in a food processor (or bash with a rolling pin in a bag) and add to the pan.

- Purée the berries in a liquidiser or food processor (or rub through a sieve) then sieve to remove the pips and set aside.

- Line a baking sheet with nonstick baking paper and divide the biscuit mixture between 4 x 10 cm (4 in) ring moulds, pressing down well. Chill until needed.

- To make the filling, whisk together the cream cheese, sugar, lemon zest and juice and vanilla extract. Sprinkle the gelatine into the measured water in a small bowl and microwave on high for 30 seconds. Mix a little of the cheese mixture into the gelatine, then stir the gelatine back into the cheese mixture.

- Meanwhile, whisk the cream to soft peaks and fold into the cheese mixture with the berry purée and swirl gently to create a marbled effect. Pour into the moulds and flatten with a palette knife. Chill until ready to serve.

- To serve, release the cakes from the moulds by running a knife around the edge. Decorate with berries and mint leaves.

 ### 10 Boozy Chocolate and Berry Pots

Melt 75 g (3 oz) dark chocolate in a saucepan and stir in 150 g (5 oz) fresh mixed berries. In a bowl, whisk 200 g (7 oz) cream cheese with 3 tablespoons brandy and 25 g (1 oz) caster sugar. Spoon the chocolate mixture into the base of 4 dessert bowls and top with the cream cheese mixture. Serve chilled or at room temperature.

 ### 20 Mini Berry Cheesecake

Pavlovas Whisk together 200 g (7 oz) cream cheese with 50 g (2 oz) icing sugar and a few drops of vanilla extract. Stir 300 g (10 oz) fresh mixed berries into the cream cheese mixture and divide between 8 meringue nests. Melt 50 g (2 oz) dark chocolate in a small saucepan and drizzle this over the pavlovas. Serve immediately.

10 Mango and Mint Carpaccio

Serves 4

6 tablespoons golden
 caster sugar
finely grated zest and juice
 of 1 large lime
2 tablespoons finely chopped
 mint leaves, plus extra leaves
 to decorate
6–8 tablespoons water
4 firm, ripe mangoes
vanilla ice cream, to serve
 (optional)

- Put the sugar in a small saucepan with the lime zest and juice, mint and measured water. Bring to the boil and remove from the heat. Stir until the sugar is dissolved. Set aside to cool.

- Meanwhile, cut the mangoes in half, running a sharp knife around the stones to detach. Peel and slice as thinly as possible.

- Arrange the mango slices on 4 serving plates and drizzle with the sugar syrup.

- Serve with vanilla ice cream, if desired, and decorate with mint leaves.

2 Hot Toffee Mangoes with Lime

Heat a frying pan over a medium heat and cook 75 g (3 oz) caster sugar until it starts to melt and turn golden. Add 50 g (2 oz) butter and 2 mangoes, peeled, stoned and thickly sliced and cook for 5–6 minutes or until the mango is coated in the sugar syrup. Add the finely grated zest and juice of 1 lime then simmer for 2 minutes. Serve hot with a sprinkling of chopped mint leaves and vanilla ice cream.

3 Grilled Mango with Lime and Mint

Syrup Slowly melt 200 g (7 oz) caster sugar in a pan over a medium heat until dark amber. Remove from the heat and carefully add 100 ml (3½ fl oz) lime juice and 4 tablespoons finely chopped mint. Return to the heat and stir until the caramel melts again. Cool and set aside until needed. Beat 250 g (8 oz) mascarpone, 150 ml (¼ pint) coconut cream and 3 tablespoons icing sugar together until smooth. Chill until required. Cut 4 ripe mangoes into 'mango cheeks': hold the mango vertically and, using a sharp knife, cut down both sides of the stone. Sprinkle 2 tablespoons caster sugar on to the cut side of the mango cheeks, shaking off any excess. Grill on a nonstick griddle pan, cut side down, for 4–5 minutes. Arrange the mango cheeks on a plate, grilled side up. Serve with coconut cream mixture and drizzle over the syrup.

Index

Page references in *italics*
indicate photographs.

Acknowledgements

Editorial director: **Eleanor Maxfield**
Copy editor: **Nikki Sims**
Design concept and layout: **www.gradedesign.com**
Art editors: **Juliette Norsworthy & Mark Kan**
Photographer: **Will Heap**
Food stylist: **Sunil Vijayakar**
Stylist: **Isabel De Cordova**
Senior production manager: **Katherine Hockley**